# DOCWRA'S
# DERRY

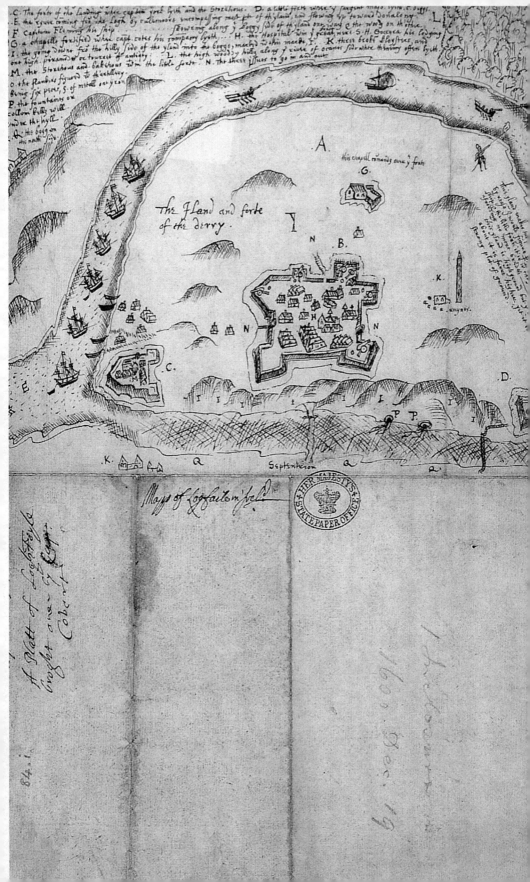

# DOCWRA'S DERRY

*A Narration of Events in
North-west Ulster*

1600–1604

*Edited in 1849 by*
John O'Donovan

*This edition edited by*
William Kelly

ULSTER HISTORICAL
FOUNDATION

The Ulster Historical Foundation is pleased to acknowledge support for this publication given by Derry City Council and
The Honourable The Irish Society

FRONTISPIECE

Contemporary sketch plan of Derry dated 27 December 1600.
This is the oldest known map of Derry (Public Record Office, London).

Published 2003, reprinted 2008
by Ulster Historical Foundation
Cotton Court, 30–42 Waring Street, Belfast, BT1 2ED
www.ancestryireland.com

© William Kelly
ISBN 978-1-903688-22-9

Design by Dunbar Design

# CONTENTS

*This book is dedicated*

*to the memory of*

*Dermot Francis*

*a defender of Derry*

*and of our shared heritage*

# ACKNOWLEDGEMENTS

As editor of this new edition of Sir Henry Docwra's *Narration*, I owe a number of debts of gratitude for help and encouragement during the compilation of the volume. First and foremost our thanks are due to Derry City Council Cultural Affairs Committee, whose publication subvention made this project possible. An especial word of gratitude is due in this regard to Mr Dermot Francis and his staff at Museum Services. The library staff at the Magee Campus of the University of Ulster gave freely of their time to track down manuscripts and obscure references. The staff of the Institute for Ulster-Scots Studies, in particular Mrs Mary Delargy and Dr Karen Stapleton, should be applauded for their diligence in assisting the editor. The Director of the Institute, Professor John Wilson, was always a source of support and encouragement.

The present edition could not have come to print without the meticulous typing skills of Gina McKinney, who transferred Sir Henry Docwra's text to computer and is deserving of a particular mention here. The completed Introduction was read by a number of colleagues and I am grateful to Hiram Morgan, Peter Smith, Eamon Ó Ciardha and John McGurk for all their comments and very useful criticisms. This volume would not have been so reader-friendly were it not for the expertise of Amanda McMullan of the University of Ulster's Academy for Irish Cultural Heritages, who produced the maps to accompany it.

Fintan Mullan and the staff of the Ulster Historical Foundation are to be congratulated not only for their role as publishers but for their forbearance of the editor's foibles. Finally, I bear an especial debt of gratitude to Ellen Whelan for her constant support.

W.P. KELLY
SEPTEMBER 2003

# PREFACE

DERRY CITY COUNCIL have commissioned this new edition of Sir Henry Docwra's *Narration of the Services done by the Army Ymployed to Lough-Foyle* to mark the granting of the first city charter by James VI/I in 1604. It is also apposite that this volume appears at the 400th anniversary of the Treaty of Mellifont in March 1603. We are truly fortunate that Sir Henry left us a full and remarkable record of 'the services done by the army ymployed to Lough-Foyle, vnder the leadinge of mee'. The *Narration*, which has an intrinsic value far beyond the merely local, has only once been published before this present edition. In 1849 John O'Donovan recognised its importance and reprinted it in *The Miscellany of the Celtic Society*. O'Donovan's edition is no longer widely accessible to the public, and it is hoped that this edition will make these important events more widely known.

Docwra's account details the military operations of the army sent by Elizabeth I to capture north-west Ulster and bring to an end the Nine Years War. Written in 1614, the *Narration* is a retrospective justification for Sir Henry's actions during, and immediately after, the military campaign in the years 1600–1603. While the emphasis is on military matters, the *Narration* also includes comment on political and socio-economic conditions in Ulster at the beginning of the seventeenth century and is an invaluable source for the study of this period. The expedition to the Foyle also produced the first detailed maps of Derry and Donegal. These were on public display for the first time in the city during Derry City Council's 'Mapping the City' exhibition celebrating the Millennium in 2000.[1] The maps are particularly valuable in that they recorded for posterity the remains of the monastic settlements at Derry and Rathmullan and include sites now lost, such as Fahan Castle.

Docwra did not write his *Narration* until over a decade after the

1

events that it relates. The reasons why he wrote it at this time are of interest in themselves, and allow an insight into the politics of Ireland and England in the second decade of the seventeenth century. In 1614 Docwra was over 50 years old – a considerable age in the seventeenth century. He was now a career civil servant rather than soldier, and he was still ambitious. Advancement did not come easily for Docwra after the war. Although he was a Commissioner for Irish Causes he faced constant sniping from rivals and enemies within the Irish administration. Docwra had served under Elizabeth I but now James VI and I was king and a different set of courtiers held sway; new factions influenced appointments to office. By 1614 Sir Henry had his eye on the lucrative office of Treasurer at War. As part of the perennial scramble for office his rivals supported accusations of incompetence and unfitness against Docwra with long-standing aspersions concerning his management of the expedition to Lough Foyle. The *Narration*, therefore, is partly an attempt at vindicating his role in the Nine Years War but also a counterblast against his critics in the administration.

The reader should bear in mind that the *Narration* was written with a view to explaining *ex post facto* what had occurred over ten years previously. It was also written to explain events that had occurred since that time which might be used by enemies to denigrate Docwra's management of the enterprise and, more importantly, his contemporary fitness for office. During the course of the war Docwra had been variously, and consistently, accused of incompetence, naivety about or lenience towards the Irish, the embezzlement of crown finances, and self-promotion at the expense of his officers. The *Narration* specifically rebuts these accusations. Sir Henry is always at pains to point out that it was his army that cut Ó Néill off from his allies in north-west Ulster, that his policies toward the Irish were governed by specific instructions from Whitehall, that he could at all times fully account for expenditure and that the interest of the crown was his paramount motivation. Although his own officers often differ in their estimation of Docwra's competence or his military effectiveness, none contradict the merely factual outline of the campaign in Ulster.

One particular accusation – that he was too lenient with the Irish – is rebutted by Docwra throughout the *Narration*. This apparent failing gained more currency after the revolt of his client and protégé, Sir Cathaír Ó Dochartaigh, in 1608, in the course of which he sacked and burnt the town that Docwra had established at Derry. In the

*Narration* Sir Henry constantly refers to how the Irish could not have been defeated without a much greater expenditure in blood and money had they not been set at each other's throats on behalf of the English. The *Narration* is also Docwra's defiant assertion of how he was sold short, in his mind, by the state and by officers he trusted after the Treaty of Mellifont in 1603. Charles Blount, Lord Mountjoy, Docwra's superior and later earl of Devonshire is singled out in the text, by unsubtle implication rather than direct accusation, as a man who failed to keep his promises to Sir Henry in particular but also to his Irish allies. Docwra was embittered at what he thought was the meagre reward offered for his services in the wars, and he was passed over in favour of others who had more influence with the new king James VI and I.

At the same time as his *Narration* Docwra also published a laudatory tract on the career of Sir Richard Bingham (1528–99), his former commanding officer. Docwra obviously believed his own situation to be akin to that of the notorious Bingham, whom Lord Deputy Perrot had removed from his office as governor of Connacht. (Docwra was refused this same office under Essex.) In 1592 Lord Deputy Perrot 'formally complained to the queen of Bingham's habitual severity and insubordination', and recommended that he be removed from office. As Docwra would do later, Bingham fled to court to plead his case but was immediately imprisoned for leaving his post without licence.[2] However, to judge by Sir Henry Docwra's tract and his behaviour during the war in Ulster, Bingham was something of a role model for Docwra. Moreover, Docwra doubtless saw his own misfortunes reflected in the fate of the detested Sir Richard. The ingratitude of the state, accusations of mismanagement, politically expedient dismissal, and the disregard of former friends at court all contributed to his fall from grace. In Docwra's mind, and in his *Narration*, there is a striking similarity between his own treatment at court after the end of the war and that meted out Bingham in 1592. We should not perhaps credit Sir Henry with too much subtlety, but there is a certain irony in the fact that Bingham, Docwra's mentor as a young soldier, was dismissed for precisely the opposite accusation – severity – to that levelled at Docwra with regard to his treatment of the Irish. Moreover, reports of Docwra's 'leniency' would have come as a surprise to the Irish, many thousands of whom died at the hands of his soldiers or starved to death in a deliberately induced famine.

Significantly, however, Docwra's disagreement with Mountjoy arose especially because of what he saw as the leniency of the lord deputy towards the defeated Irish lords. Sir Henry could not stomach the new political dispensation in Ulster, where his former enemies were now restored to their positions of power. Docwra was always at heart a soldier rather than a politician. Excessively cosy relations with some of the Irish and too deep-seated a hatred of Ó Néill and Ó Domhnaill meant that he was not the man to govern a conquered Ulster. He may have won the war but, as far as Mountjoy and his faction at court were concerned – and Sir Henry admits as much in his *Narration* – he was not the man to manage the peace. The *Narration*, therefore, has as much to do with politics post-1603 as it has with the events it relates, and is essentially Docwra's defence of his generalship during the Nine Years War and his application for promotion in 1614. In 1616 he was appointed Treasurer at War in Ireland.

After his death Docwra's account, and his life, attracted little attention apart from that of professional historians. We are indeed fortunate that John O'Donovan (1809–61) took the trouble to copy and publish the *Narration* in 1849. He was in fact ideally placed to do so, having worked in Ulster for the Ordnance Survey.[3] A lawyer and Irish scholar, O'Donovan was singularly gifted as a translator and editor. He published the *Narration* while he was translating and editing the *Annals of the Four Masters* (1848–51) and was therefore acquainted with both Irish and English accounts of these events. His work for the Ordnance Survey and his scholarship gave him an extensive knowledge of the place-names and personal names which allowed him to identify and translate into Irish those often crudely rendered in English by Docwra. One of the most valuable contributions of O'Donovan's edition is his identification of place names and their meanings in Irish, included in the text of his notes. These are reprinted in full here. O'Donovan's original endnotes for the *Narration* are also reproduced here unaltered, except for the references to the pages in the new text and on those few occasions where the present editor has felt it necessary to correct errors.

Docwra's language obviously seems archaic to modern ears, and can at times be somewhat obscure. His idiosyncratic spelling is characteristic of his time. That said, Docwra had a soldier's hand and his *Narration* reads, naturally enough, like a military report. Nonetheless, the uninhibited plain style of the *Narration* conveys his determination to tell, according to his recollection, exactly what happened, even some 14 years after the event. The *Narration* certainly repays the effort required initially. This edition provides some assistance for the general reader. A glossary of terms, glossary of names, chronology, maps and an introduction will, it is hoped, assist in guiding the reader through the text.

The text of the *Narration* as produced by O'Donovan in 1849 has not been altered in any way, and is reproduced here in full. All dates in the text have been modernised in that the year begins in January rather than on Lady Day, 25 March, as was the convention in the seventeenth century. All personal Irish names in the introduction are given as they are spelt in the vernacular rather than in English translation.

1  State Papers Ireland, SP63, vols 241–60, Map of part of Inishowen: PRO SP63/207 Part VI, no. 84 (i). Reproduced in Hayes McCoy, G.A., (ed.), *Ulster and Other Irish Maps circa 1600*, Irish Manuscripts Commission, Dublin, 1964. *CSPI*, November 1600–July 1601, p. 339 gives the name of the mapmaker as Robert Ashby and the number as 71, iv.

2  In his notes on Docwra's relation of Bingham's career, John O'Donovan cites O'Flaherty's *Chorographical Description of West Connaught* to the effect that Sir Richard was 'universally detested by the native Irish, who considered him a sanguinary monster ... and full dearly did he make them pay for the imputation'. O'Donovan goes on to explain that Bingham was removed from office by Elizabeth I on Lord Deputy Perrot's advice when it was deemed politic at court to pacify Ireland at a time when England's attention had turned to the wars in France. As O'Donovan explains it, the queen, 'hearing that Sir Richard Bingham had hanged too many of the nobility of the province of Connacht ... understanding that it was impossible to reconcile the Irish to him, contrived to have him removed as if to please the Irish' (O'Donovan, J. (ed.) 'Docwra's relation', *Miscellany of the Celtic Society*, pp. 214–15, 227 (Dublin, 1849); *Chorographical Description of West Connaught*, Hardiman, J. (ed.), (Dublin, 1846).

3  One of the most interesting exhibitions in Derry City Council's Tower Museum narrates the story of the Ordnance Survey and its staff. The Survey team were referred to, quite rightly, as 'a peripatetic university'. The intention was to publish a series of volumes on the areas surveyed but only one in fact emerged: that for the Parish of Templemore in Londonderry.

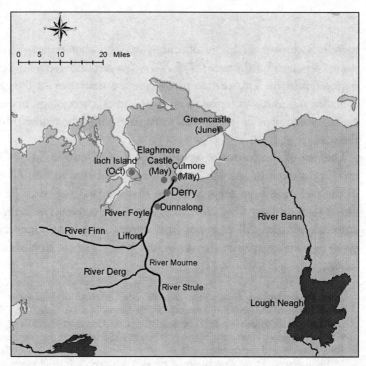

Map of north-west Ulster showing the military campaign in 1600.

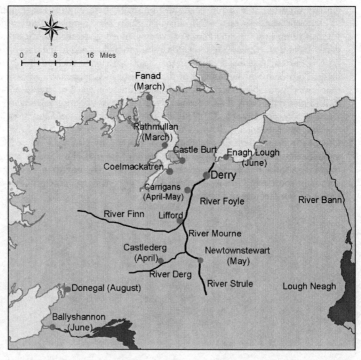

Map of north-west Ulster showing the military campaign in 1601.

# INTRODUCTION

IN THE MIDDLE OF MAY 1600 a fleet of English warships and transports carrying over 4,000 soldiers approached 'the Derrie', an island situated in the River Foyle in Ulster. For the men on board the ships this was *terra incognita*, a land so unknown they might well have been in the Americas. They knew one thing for certain. They would not be made welcome.[1] They had come to Ireland to plant a garrison in a country at war with their queen, a place where they would be surrounded by enemies. In the course of the war so far, successive English armies had been defeated or destroyed on at least four occasions, and in 1599 the Irish had even forced the ignominious departure of the queen's favourite, the Earl of Essex, who had been sent to Ireland with an army of almost 20,000 men.[2]

Over a decade later, the commander of the expedition to Lough Foyle set down an account of his campaign in north-west Ulster. The tale he tells is history on the heroic scale: a story of courage and cowardice, honour and dishonour, fidelity and betrayal, humanity and brutality. It is the story of a terrible war, the end of an era in the history of Ireland and the beginning of another, the destruction of a society and the foundation of a new city. It is an account of three wars: an imperialist war (the final subjection of Ulster to the crown of England and the end of Spanish attempts to use Ireland as the back door to England); a religious war fought on a European scale (the ideological clash of Protestantism and Catholicism); and above all, and most tragically, a civil war between the Irish themselves.[3]

In January 1600 Sir Henry Docwra was appointed 'Chief Commander and Governor of all Her Majesty's forces of horse and foot assigned for Lough Foyle'. Docwra was an excellent choice of commander. At 36 years of age he was a seasoned veteran of military campaigns against the Spanish in the Netherlands and against the

7

Irish in Connacht.[4] He had arrived in Ireland in the previous year as colonel of a regiment serving under the Earl of Essex, who proposed to promote him to the governorship of Connacht.[5] Nothing came of the proposal, and on his return to England in disgrace late that year Essex took Docwra with him, ostensibly to have his patent as governor confirmed, but also perhaps to have someone on hand to help explain his dismal military record in Ireland.[6] Docwra managed to escape the blame apportioned in this affair, and in January of the following year he was given command of the expedition to Lough Foyle.[7]

This expedition was not the first Elizabeth I had sent to north-west Ulster. The strategic importance of the Foyle became very apparent during Seán Ó Néill's rebellion in the 1560s, and an expedition was dispatched there in September 1566.[8] Seven companies of foot and a troop of horse under the command of Sir Edward Randolph (or Randoll) were sent to Derry with the intention of fortifying the island as part of Lord Deputy Sidney's campaign against Ó Néill. After some initial successes against the Irish, Randolph was killed in November in a skirmish near Muff. A winter in Derry soon reduced the small garrison through illness, but their morale was completely shattered when their remaining stores were destroyed in April by the explosion of the powder magazine located in the Templemore.[9] The survivors, ravaged by disease, were withdrawn.

Seán Ó Néill's rebellion collapsed with his death in 1567, but in the last decade of the century a rebellion much more deadly to England's interests led by much more capable men than the headstrong Seán broke out in Ulster. During what has become known as the Nine Years War, Aodh Ó Néill, Earl of Tyrone and Aodh Ruadh Ó Domhnaill allied together to maintain their independence in Ulster. This alliance ended centuries of rivalry between the two great clans and presented their enemies with a formidable challenge. The problem for the English forces was that to defeat Ó Néill and Ó Domhnaill they had to capture their power base in the almost impenetrable mountains and forests of Derry, Donegal, Tyrone and Fermanagh. The plan, first mooted in the 1560s, of attacking on three fronts was now reactivated with more determination. Sir Arthur Chichester would harry the Irish from Carrickfergus in the east, Docwra would attack into Inishowen and Co. Derry in the west, and Lord Deputy Mountjoy would push into rebel territory from the south-east through the Moyry Pass. This time the English were intent on staying.[10]

By the time their forces arrived in the Foyle, the Nine Years War had entered the fifth year of conflict. Exasperated by the tenacity of the Irish, who had already seen off a number of armies and were bleeding her exchequer, Elizabeth I resolved to end the war once and for all. On the advice of Charles Blount, Lord Mountjoy, she equipped an invasion fleet for Derry. Strategically, Docwra's priority was to outflank the Earl of Tyrone by cutting off his base of supply in Ulster. Another force, under the command of Sir Mathew Morgan, was to capture Ballyshannon and drive a wedge between Cenél Eoghain and their Ó Domhnaill allies in Tyrconnel. These tactics would also cut the Irish off from their allies in Scotland and Spain. Moreover, experience had shown that the Irish lack of modern artillery made it exceptionally difficult for them to overrun garrisons in well-fortified strong points. Resupply by sea made these fortified camps almost self-sufficient, and from their secure bases the English could lay waste the countryside.[11]

Docwra's tactics are clearly set out in his *Narration*. He followed, almost to the letter, the blueprint set out the previous year by military planners.[12] In the first place he set about establishing a series of strong-points to command the surrounding countryside, something that can be accomplished using relatively few troops. He hoped to achieve this by capturing strategic castles from the Irish, repairing abandoned castles, or building new fortifications along the lines of communication. His troops also swept the countryside, killing and burning as they went, destroying crops and livestock to induce famine.[13] The impact of these raids on a seasonal agricultural economy, to say nothing of the effect on Irish morale, could be devastating. On one raid alone, Docwra tells us, two of his officers 'took 160 cows and killed 30 people … [Captain Windsor] slew 100 of them, including three chief men of account, many kerne, the rest churls, women and children, (for he spared none)'. As part of this strategy, and to open up a route into the heartland of the Tyrone lordship, Docwra attacked across the Foyle into the Ó Catháin's territories (Oireacht Uí Chatháin) in Co. Derry. Perhaps most importantly, the English attempted to draw as many of the Irish as possible over to their side.[14] This tactic was to have profound consequences not only on the course of the war in Ulster but for Gaelic society in the years to come.

Docwra's most important priority was to establish a base at Derry from which he could launch attacks and be resupplied from England.[15] Even as the ships arrived in the Foyle, however, they had an indication of the opposition they would meet when they ran aground and immediately came under fire from musketeers on the shore. Two days later, with only token resistance from the garrison, he secured the fort of Culmore guarding the narrow passage from Lough Foyle into the river.[16] He left 600 men as a garrison and sent reconnaissance parties to the castle at Elaghmore abandoned earlier by Muintir Uí Dhochartaigh. The English seized Derry unopposed on 22 May.[17]

What they captured was a ruin. Little was left of the monastic settlement, much of which had been destroyed during Randolph's earlier occupation[18] (see map). According to Sir Henry, all that remained standing was the ruins of the old abbey, a bishop's house, two churches and an old castle.[19] However, the site had been well chosen by its previous inhabitants. Docwra remarked that the location was a natural fortress bounded by the river and with steep embankments on three sides, lying 'in the form of a bow bent, whereof the bog is the string and the river the bow'. There were ample building materials to hand in the ruins of the settlement, and woods and quarries on or near the site. Much to the disgust of the local Irish, the English demolished the remaining buildings, desecrating what remained of 'the great saint' Colmcille's monastery by eating and sleeping in the ruins.[20] Apart from attacking foraging parties, the Irish by and large left the newcomers alone. They had few forces in the area, the majority having been drawn off by Mountjoy's diversionary attack to give Docwra time to establish a bridgehead on the Foyle.[21] In any case the Irish remembered the fate of the previous garrison and preferred to wait until conditions had weakened their enemy. Docwra too was very conscious of the disastrous outcome of Randolph's expedition, and immediately set about building quarters for his men. At his insistence, his force had sufficient carpenters and masons to accomplish the task.[22]

Two substantial forts, later known as the Upper and Lower Forts, were built immediately. The Upper Fort stood to the south-west of the island citadel, roughly where the Bishop's Palace was later built and extended towards what is now the Long Tower chapel. The Lower Fort was positioned at the northern approaches in the area previously occupied by an Ó Dochartaigh tower house. Well aware of the havoc wreaked on the health of the previous garrison by an Irish winter, Docwra was given strict orders in his warrant to build a hospital, the costs of which were to be defrayed from the soldiers' wages.[23] Soon after the English began what operations they could by raiding into Inishowen. Sir Henry's stay in Ireland was almost cut short at the end of July when he was so badly injured in an engagement with the Irish that there were fears he would not survive.[24] In fact, the Earl of Ormonde recommended the Lord Deputy 'to consider of a meet man out of hand to be sent to Lough Foyle to take charge there, if Sir Henry Dockwra should miscarry, which I greatly fear'.[25] Sir Henry 'kepte my Bedd of this wound by the space of a fortneth, my chamber a weeke after'.

Little military action of any note occurred while Docwra was unable to take direct command in the field, but, even though the English suffered few casualties from enemy action, disease had already taken hold in the garrison. It seemed to Docwra that his main enemy was not so much the Irish as Ireland itself. The inclement weather even in August – which, Sir Henry lamented, had to be seen to be believed – took an enormous toll of men. By the end of the month the garrison had no masons or carpenters left, all having perished through illness. Insanitary conditions contributed enormously to the spread of illness, often contracted because the men were forced to drink water rather than beer.[26] Fearing that these losses would be blamed on his mismanagement, Docwra ascribed the mortality to the 'distemperature of the air'. Sir Henry's astonishment at summer weather in Ulster is apparent in his appeal to the Privy Council that 'Our men daily fall down beyond expectation and almost all credit. The weather is already grown wonderful stormy, even such as no man can conceive that feeleth it not.'[27] By the beginning of September he had 'seas of sick men that daily increased, some by wilful idleness, some by mere counterfeiting, some by hurts and other casualties, and others by the hand of God'. Such was the condition of the men that a hardened veteran like Docwra admitted that it 'made even my soul to grieve'.[28] Some were deserting to the Irish, carrying intelligence and even going so far as to encourage them to attack their former comrades in their state of weakness.[29] The poor condition of his troops induced Docwra to hold his ground over the winter while doing what he could to block supply routes into Inishowen by garrisoning Dunnalong, Colmackatren and Carrigans.[30]

The Irish tactic of standing off and letting disease do its work among the garrison, which had previously served them very well, had obvious advantages but left the initiative with the English. In

11

September, therefore, Ó Domhnaill attacked, presumably on receipt of the news that Docwra expected reinforcements from England. The attack failed and he withdrew, leaving sufficient forces to block the garrison up and protect the Inishowen peninsula. While Inishowen remained unconquered behind him Docwra could not afford to attack Muintir Uí Chatháin in Co. Derry. The turning point came in October, when Niall Garbh Ó Domhnaill came in to Derry and pledged allegiance to the queen. This was a godsend for Docwra, a major fissure in the rebel alliance. On information supplied by one of his spies, 'an Irish priest', Sir Geoffrey Fenton explained to the Secretary of State, Sir Robert Cecil, the circumstances behind the defection:

> Niall Garbh Ó Domhnaill and his men, in a drunken fury upon an old grudge, murdered one Neachtan Ó Domhnaill, Niall's own uncle, a man of great authority with Niall Ó Domhnaill and all his country. Whereupon Niall, fearing Niall Ó Domhnaill's revenge at his return from Thomond and Connaught (whither he and O'Ruairc were gone to make a prey) withdrew himself, his creaghts and followers, into a strong corner of the country belonging to Sir Seán Ó Dochartaigh.[31]

Niall Garbh also 'wrought Sir John O'Dogherty to be one of the party'.[32] Fenton jubilantly told Cecil that 'Out of the revolt of Neale Garve your Honour may see how God doth work for Her Majesty; which no doubt doth more astonish the confederates of the north than if 1,000 of them had fallen by the edge of the Queen's sword.'[33] With Inishowen secured, the English at Derry were now free to inflict the horrors of 'frightfulness' on the lordship of Ó Catháin. However, neither Sir Henry nor his second-in-command, Sir John Bolles, trusted Ó Dochartaigh, fearing that his defection had been prompted merely by a desire to protect his lands, something he could not do without assistance from Ó Domhnaill. Their suspicions were confirmed when it was reported that Ó Dochartaigh was planning to seize Culmore and Elaghmore in concert with Ó Domhnaill.[34] Docwra's spy was instructed to win their confidence and invite Sir Seán and Aodh Buidhe Mac Daibhéid to a dinner, with the intention of killing them both.

As it turned out, Sir Henry was saved the trouble of murdering the chieftain by his convenient death at Christmas 1600. This unexpected event entirely changed the circumstances of the Ó Dochartaigh clan. The heir apparent was the young and inexperienced Cathaír, who would inevitably be guided by older and wiser counsels. Fearing his defection, Aodh Ruadh Ó Domhnaill had seized and imprisoned him as soon as the English landed, but was later persuaded to release him into the custody of Aodh Buidhe and Feidhlim Ruadh Ó Dochartaigh.[35] Almost immediately Muintir Uí Dhochartaigh defected to the English. By bringing in Muintir Uí Dhochartaigh Docwra had achieved one of the major aims of the expedition to Derry. Drawing Irish clans away from their loyalty to Cenél Eoghain and Clann Dálaigh was an integral and essential part of the English plan to suppress Ulster. An explicit part of the rationale of planting a garrison of such strength at Derry was to 'give comfort to the Irish to draw to them, of whom … many will come in, when they see the garrison strong to defend them'.[36] Even before the English had arrived in the Foyle, while they were still at Carrickfergus, Sir Art Ó Néill and Sir Seán Ó Dochartaigh had intimated that they would assist Docwra.[37]

By this stage, in the middle of winter, the English garrison was already in dire straits. What saved the day for Docwra was dissensions among the Irish themselves and the defection of Niall Garbh Ó Domhnaill in particular. In his *Narration* and correspondence, Docwra was forthright in asserting that his defection to the English 'was very acceptable att that time, & such as wee made many vses of, & could have ill spared'. The motivation of the Irish in joining the English is explained by Docwra as a desire for 'priuate Revenge' although he candidly admits that, as instructed, he made 'vse of them for the furtherance of the Publique seruice' (*Narration* p.52).

Locked in their encampment, the English were almost blind without the intelligence the Irish provided. Without Irish help Docwra could not have advanced as quickly or wrought as much havoc among his enemies. For example, Docwra's purpose in planting garrisons in all the small castles he captured was to 'Spoyle & pray them of theire Catle, & that impossible to be done without intelligence & Guidance of some of the Natiues' (*Narration* p.58). Moreover, many of the Irish made convenient alliances with the more powerful English forces when there was no opportunity to resist. Niall Garbh later argued with some justice to the Privy Council in Dublin that Ireland had not been conquered by the English but by his own arms.[38] On many occasions the Irish actually bore the brunt of the fighting: a bonus, one

English commentator remarked, since it removed those they might eventually have to fight themselves. Indeed, one of the criteria for receiving the queen's pardon, according to Fynes Moryson, was that 'he never received any to mercy, but such as had drawn blood on their fellow-rebels'.

Although they were undoubtedly crucial to the success of his campaign, Sir Henry often despaired of the loyalty of his Irish troops. He was acutely aware that only his own power and their own adverse circumstances at the time bound them to his cause, suspecting, quite rightly in a number of cases, that they would immediately revert to their previous allegiance if the circumstances of the English changed for the worse. On one occasion he told the Privy Council in exasperation that 'their perfidiousness, discontentment, and secret affection for their own country, is such as a thousand times I wish they had never been entertained'.[39] The queen's officers in Ireland and England were acutely conscious that Irish compliance was often a temporary measure and brought the Irish considerable reward. While in rebellion, the Privy Council complained, they could apparently sustain themselves without difficulty, but 'we do see it is a common thing nowadays, that when such a one as Sir Art Ó Néill or Ó Dochartaigh is a rebel, they are able to live and infest the Queen, but when they come in, the Queen is put to an extreme charge, as though she commanded no country beyond the trenches'.[40]

Clearly, some of Docwra's 'allies' passed intelligence on the condition of the English to Ó Domhnaill and his officers. They were aware by the middle of September 1600 that Docwra had less than a fifth of his force in any condition to fight and sufficient supplies for less than a week. It was at this juncture the Irish made their most determined attempt yet on the garrison, attacking with over 2,000 men from the Bogside. Only the vigilance of the guard saved the English from being overwhelmed. On the following day fresh supply arrived from England, and soon after reinforcements of 50 cavalry and 600 foot.

Within two weeks of these events, however, the defection of Niall Garbh Ó Domhnaill to the English completely changed the balance of power. The accession of Niall Garbh and his followers gave Docwra the opportunity to expand his operations against the Irish in Inishowen and Tyrconnel. At the end of the first week of October Sir John Bolles was despatched with 500 foot and a troop of cavalry to support Niall Garbh in an attack on Lifford. Faced by such odds, the small garrison fled but Aodh Ruadh counter-attacked quickly by moving forces close to the town and launching a half-hearted assault on 12 October. The Irish closely invested Lifford for two weeks thereafter to prevent the English from ravaging the surrounding countryside and destroying the harvest.[41] On 24 October, on the advice of Niall Garbh, the garrison sallied out in strength and drove the Irish from the field. Among those killed, reputedly by Niall himself, was Maghnus Ó Domhnaill, younger brother of the Ó Domhnaill.[42] Niall Garbh's future now lay irrevocably with the English, since Aodh Ruadh would certainly avenge the death of his younger brother.[43]

By mid-November the Irish had broken off the investment of Lifford. Sir Henry reported that both Aodh Ruadh and the Earl of Tyrone had marched on the 10th of the month to meet Spanish vessels expected at Killybegs carrying munitions and money. The Spaniards landed arms and money at Teelin Bay in December 1600 and arrived at Killybegs in the following month. Docwra took the opportunity to let Niall Garbh and Sir John Bolles loose, raiding the east bank of the Foyle with, as Sir Henry freely confessed, apparently little military consequence: '[the Irish] had theire owne ends in it, which were always for priuate Revenge, & we ours to make vse of them for the furtherance of the Publique seruice' (*Narration* p.52).

The death of the venerable Sir Seán Ó Dochartaigh at Christmas 1600 improved Docwra's tactical situation immeasurably by bringing the entire Ó Dochartaigh sept, and therefore all of Inishowen, over to his side. Once again, dynastic disputes among the Irish were at the root of dissension between Muintir Dhochartaigh and Aodh Ruadh Ó Domhnaill. Immediately after the death of Sir Seán, Ó Domhnaill installed his own candidate, Feidhlim Óg, as chief of the Ó Dochartaigh sept. Two of the most eminent of Sir Seán's advisors, Aodh Buidhe and Feidhlim Ruadh Mac Daibhéid, took great exception to the exclusion of Cathaír Ó Dochartaigh, who had been their foster child. During a series of tripartite and apparently labyrinthine negotiations between Muintir Dhochartaigh and Docwra and Muintir Dhochartaigh and Ó Domhnaill, Aodh Ruadh was finally persuaded to release Cathaír and agree to his chieftainship of the clan. After agreeing their demands with Sir Henry, the Lord Deputy and Privy Council, Muintir Dhochartaigh declared for the English. The importance of this defection could hardly be overstated, and in fact Sir Henry wrote that without the help he received thereafter from

Muintir Uí Dhochartaigh, 'I must freelie confess a truth, it had been vtterlie impossible wee could haue made that sure & speedie Progress in the Warres that afterwardes wee did'[44] (*Narration* p.54). Nevertheless, there is some evidence that the Ó Dochartaigh's defection was an elaborate ruse to preserve Inishowen from the ravages of the English as a granary and storehouse for Spanish troops whom Ó Néill and Ó Domhnaill, at that stage, expected to land at Killybegs. One early casualty of the Ó Dochartaigh's apparent change of heart was the elderly Bishop of Derry, Réamonn Ó Gallchobhair, who was forced to flee his sanctuary at Fahan Castle and cross into Ó Catháin's lands in Co. Derry. The bishop was a wanted man: he had for many years acted as envoy of the Ulster Irish to the court of Spain. Late in the evening of Ash Wednesday the bishop's party was intercepted by troops under the command of Sir John Bolles and Réamonn Ó Gallchobhair was hacked to death on the spot. His companions suffered a similar fate. Thus died the last Roman Catholic Bishop of Derry until 1766. An exultant Bolles informed Secretary Cecil that 'The Bishop of Derry who is said to be the first and chief contriver of this general defection and combination with the Spaniards and has himself been thrice at Rome and oft in Spain to negotiate, God gave into my hand upon Ash Wednesday at night, but, before I could come to him, the soldiers had slain him.'[45]

Undoubtedly the Irish expected that the winter of 1600–1 would pass without much activity on either side, as it was almost customary in early modern warfare to retreat into fortified encampments to sit out the cold weather. One novel feature of this campaign was that the English embarked on a series of local raids, harassing their enemies throughout the winter months and allowing few opportunities to rest and regroup. Docwra renewed full-scale warfare in the spring of 1601 by attacking the lordship of Mac Suibhne Fánad to the west of Inishowen. Quite rightly judging that the English threat of immediate destruction outweighed the wrath of Ó Domhnaill, the Mac Suibhne promised allegiance to the queen, a decision prompted in great part by Docwra's return of most of the cattle and goods taken by his troops. A cautious Sir Henry left a garrison at Rathmullan Abbey under Captain Ralph Bingley to keep a wary eye on Fanad and in the following month moved with the bulk of his forces towards Ó Néill's lands in Tyrone.

Through the good offices of Niall Garbh, Castlederg was delivered up to him without a shot being fired. With Fanad subdued for the time being and Inishowen neutralised by the accession of Muintir Dhochartaigh, Sir Henry decided to deny Ó Domhnaill any opportunity of raiding north by building a series of small forts across the base of the Inishowen peninsula from Carrigans to Coelmacatraen (Castleforward). When Ó Domhnaill attempted to force a passage he was heavily defeated near Castleforward on 7 May. Within a fortnight of this reverse the English, reinforced with 800 fresh troops, again moved south into Tyrone and captured Newtownstewart after bombarding the castle and bawn. Docwra rapidly became aware that Irish tower houses could not withstand fire from modern artillery. Indeed, it seems that the morale of the Irish soldiers also crumbled in the face of such weaponry. Within a month the Ó Catháin's stronghold at Enagh Lough near Derry suffered the same fate as Newtownstewart. Docwra took the castle unopposed when the small garrison fled overnight after a day's battery from English cannon.

Soon after, Lord Deputy Mountjoy ordered Docwra to move his forces towards Dungannon and rendezvous with him to co-ordinate an attack on Ballyshannon, thereby opening a route into Tyrconnel. The capture of Ballyshannon had been a prime objective of the expedition but had been delayed by the untimely death of Sir Mathew Morgan. Sir Henry set in train preparations for what would undoubtedly be a hard-fought march through enemy territory. As part of his preparations he summoned his quartermaster to give an account of the available stores, particularly powder for the muskets. Satisfied that he had sufficient powder available he made ready to leave, only to discover that his force had very little store of match, a vitally important component of the matchlock muskets, without which the weapons were all but useless. Greatly embarrassed, he was forced to inform the Lord Deputy that he could not obey the order to meet him on the Blackwater.[46] In his *Narration* Docwra goes to great pains to explain this incident, and for good reason.[47] Not only was his professionalism impugned by his apparent inability to carry out a direct order at so crucial a stage in the campaign, but also the incident was seized upon by rivals in his own camp to launch a sustained lobby at court to have him removed from office.

Ever since the army had arrived at Derry, a number of officers had consistently complained about Sir Henry's management of the expedition. Sources other than the *Narration* make it plain that Docwra was disliked by almost all his subordinates. More worryingly for Docwra, some of his critics had friends at court.[48] In fact, the aptly named Sir Humphrey Covert was specifically employed on the expedition by Cecil to spy on Docwra and report back directly to the Secretary of State.[49] Much of the argument was essentially haggling over money, although couched in accusations about Sir Henry's military incompetence, and leniency or naivety about the true intentions of the Irish that had come in. Of the often contradictory accusations against Docwra, the main ones were that he had not constructed appropriate lodgings for the garrison or kept sufficient food stores, that the musters were not properly kept, too much money was spent on victualling his forces, he allowed his soldiers to be debilitated by drinking water rather than beer, and he had not provided a proper hospital.[50] There were continual arguments between Docwra and some of his officers about the numbers of troops in the muster lists of the companies and about payments to their officers. The Secretary of State warned Docwra not to request pay for 4,000 men when the queen had agreed only 3,000.

Whatever the truth or otherwise of these accusations, a few of the loudest complainants were his most senior officers. In September 1600, when Docwra sent Sir John Bolles to England to lobby for more men and supplies, Bolles took the opportunity to complain about his leadership.[51] After the Lord Deputy threw his considerable weight behind Docwra, 'one of the most sufficient men for that place [Governor of Derry] that was thought of', and defended his strategy and tactics, Elizabeth I intervened to put an end to the bickering. Bolles and others were ordered in no uncertain terms to compose their differences and think of her service rather than their own careers. Bolles was nonetheless promised Cecil's help in future.[52]

In early August Docwra went a long way towards rescuing his credit by sending Niall Garbh with his Irish troops and 500 English to capture Donegal Abbey, one of Ó Domhnaill's main bases in Tyrconnel. This coup had the additional benefit of directly threatening Ballyshannon, the objective of Mountjoy's abortive attack in July. The abbey had more than military importance; its capture was a psychological blow, planting an English garrison, under the command of Aodh Ruadh's mortal enemy, Niall, in the heartland of his lordship. During a ferocious but failed attempt to overrun the garrison, the abbey was destroyed by an explosion on 19 September.[53]

Success at Donegal was soon overshadowed by disaster in Tyrone. The recently fortified garrisons at Newtownstewart and Castlederg were overrun in mid-September. At Newtownstewart the entire English force was put to the sword, and those at Castlederg escaped only with their lives. Docwra was also suspicious of Niall Garbh and his intentions. Although he had fought bravely and contributed significantly to the capture of Donegal, Sir Henry complained bitterly that he would not obey his orders even though he was being paid handsomely; he arrogantly behaved as if he were *the* Ó Domhnaill and could act independently of the queen's officers. He was also suspected of profiteering by stealing English cattle and blaming the insurgents. The bad blood occasioned by the resulting arguments was to have more serious consequences within the year.

More significant events elsewhere, however, brought an abrupt halt to Irish counter-attacks in Ulster. On 21 September Spanish troops under the command of Don Juan del Aguila landed at Kinsale in Co. Cork, and both Ó Néill and Ó Domhnaill marched south with the bulk of their forces to join them. From Derry, the English and their Irish allies were now free to raid extensively in both Donegal and Derry, attacking Fanad again to punish the Clann tSuibhne for their renewed allegiance to Ó Domhnaill and carrying out a scorched-earth policy on the Ó Catháin's lands across the Foyle. By late December Donegal had been resupplied and Ashrowe Abbey, a step nearer to Ballyshannon, garrisoned. There was better to come. Docwra and his men went into winter quarters at the close of the year overjoyed by the recent news from Cork that the Lord Deputy had decisively defeated the Irish and Spanish at Kinsale. The war in the following year would now take a decidedly different turn.

By March 1602 Docwra's small army was ready to take the offensive in what would now be more of a mopping-up exercise than a sustained campaign. Their first important success was the capture of Ballyshannon by Captain Digges on 25 March. English operations and attendant depredations in the Ó Catháin's territories were also beginning to wear down opposition and, on 20 April, Cú Mhaighe Ballach mac Riocaird Uí Chatháin delivered Dungiven to Docwra without a fight. In the following month the English were reinforced with 800 more men in preparation for the summer campaigning season. Reinforced, rearmed and re-equipped, Docwra set out from Lifford on 16 June to rendezvous with the Lord Deputy's army at

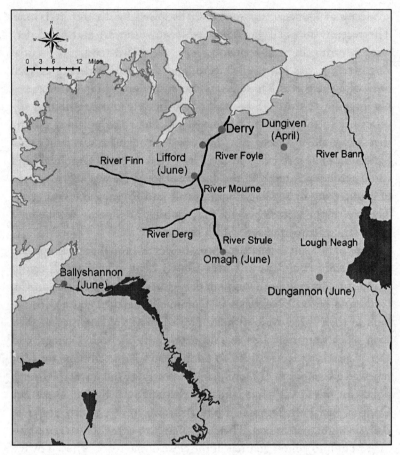

Map of north-west Ulster showing the military campaign in 1602.

Dungannon, capturing and garrisoning Omagh *en route*. Ten days later all three English armies met: Sir Arthur Chichester from Carrickfergus after marching around Lough Neagh and establishing a new fort; Docwra from Derry; and Lord Deputy Mountjoy, who immediately built Charlemont fort. This conjunction represented the success of the plan first mooted in 1599. Aodh Ó Néill was now surrounded on all sides. For Docwra this was the culmination of his work: 'the axe was now at the roote of the tree, [and] I may well say, the Necke of the Rebellion as good as vtterlie broken, for all that Tyrone was afterwardes able to doe, was but to saue himselfe in places of difficult access vnto' (*Narration* p.64).

The difficulties of access into Ó Néill's territories were greatly eased within the month. On 27 July, soon after Docwra's return to Derry, Muintir Uí Chatháin submitted to the crown. With Inishowen, much of Tyrconnel and Co. Derry now secured, Docwra again moved south to join Mountjoy in what they hoped would be the final assault against the Earl of Tyrone.

Sir Henry's elation at the surrender of Muintir Uí Chatháin was short-lived. While on his way to join the English forces, Aodh Buidhe Mac Daibhéid 'was sett upon and slaine by a partie of loose fellowes that fell vpon him by chaunce'. Docwra's sense of loss at this close ally is evident: MacDaibhéid was 'A man whome I found faithfull and honnest, let Enuie [envy] and Iguoraunce say what they will to the Contrarye' (*Narration* p.65). Within a matter of days young Catháir Ó Dochartaigh amply rewarded Docwra's trust in his Ó Dochartaigh allies by standing shoulder to shoulder with his patron when they were ambushed during a cattle raid. For this service, in which '[he] kept mee companie in the greatest heate of the feight, beheaued himselfe braulie [bravely], and with a great deale of loue and affection all that day' (*Narration* p.66), Sir Henry recommended to the Lord Deputy that the young lord be knighted.

By November 1602 resistance everywhere was beginning to fade away even at the approach of English forces. Chichester's men garrisoned Clogher and Augher, but Docwra was delayed for almost two weeks by the heroic defence of Sir Henry Hovenden's house near Newtownstewart. It is a measure of his confidence in victory by this stage that he did not even bother to garrison the castle but razed it to the ground instead. By now the Ó Domhnaill had fled to Spain, his brother had surrendered to Mountjoy and Ó Néill was isolated.

In December, English and Irish, Muintir Uí Chatháin and Muintir Uí Dhochartaigh joined forces to launch an attack on Tyrone's stronghold in the Glynnes (Glenconkeyne). It was an ignominious failure. Docwra's Irish allies refused to carry the fight into the thickly wooded valleys, and Docwra and Chichester failed to rendezvous as planned. It was then resolved to let winter do the work and starve Ó Néill out into open country in the spring, where the much superior English forces could deal with him almost at leisure. In the meantime their Irish allies could harry him with intermittent small-scale actions. The plan worked. Aodh Ó Néill, Earl of Tyrone, surrendered to Lord

Mountjoy on 30 March 1603 at Mellifont Abbey. Even years later when he penned his *Narration* Docwra remembered the joy of the occasion: 'the bussines done that wee came for, and the Warre happilie and gloriouslie ended' (*Narration* p.74).[54]

Docwra's anticipated return to a more relaxed regime in winter quarters at Derry was delayed when his troubled relationship with the fractious Niall Garbh finally boiled over in late 1602. On campaign, Sir Henry had heard rumours that his erstwhile ally had seized the provisions of the Lifford garrison. More seriously, he seized all of Rudhraighe Ó Domhnaill's cattle, which were under Crown protection, and declared himself the Ó Domhnaill at the traditional investiture site near Kilmacrennan. He probably took the title of the Ó Domhnaill hoping to present Docwra and Mountjoy with a *fait accompli*. The tactic backfired spectacularly. Incensed, Docwra sarcastically asked him when he returned to Derry 'howe he was suddenly stept into the Name of a lord [and] by what aucthoritie he was soe' (*Narration* p.71). Apprarently chastened, Niall Garbh agreed to restore all the cattle to Rudhraighe Ó Domhnaill, but on the very next day set an ambush to assassinate him while he was on his way to meet Docwra.

By this time the Earl of Tyrone had surrendered, the rebellion was quenched and Elizabeth I had died on 24 March. James VI of Scotland was now James I of England, and many in Ireland expected a new political dispensation from a monarch who was widely rumoured to favour toleration of Catholicism. Docwra feared that Niall Garbh would seize the opportunity to 'stepp aside and take Armes, thinkeing by that meanes to make his owne peace, how should I aunswere it, that haue him now in my handes ... what a Blemish would it be to all my actions, if the kinge, at his first Coming in, should finde all the kingdome quiet but onelie this litle parte vnder my Charge.' (*Narration* p.72) Sir Henry was therefore somewhat relieved to receive orders from the Lord Deputy to seize Niall Garbh for treason. On being arrested, Niall Garbh exclaimed in horror when told of the charge, 'Then I ame a dead man.' It is to Docwra's credit that he stoutly defended Niall Garbh against the capital charge, pointing out to the Lord Deputy that this treason (reviving ancient titles) was reserved in law only for the Ó Néill.[55] The prisoner was held under open arrest in the town after giving parole, but escaped three days later. Overtaken by English forces, he fled to Fanad trying to reach Doe Castle, reportedly the strongest in Ulster. Angry at Niall Garbh's broken promises, Sir Henry's resolve was 'that in his heart I was verylie [truly] perswaded hee was at that time a Malitious [malicious] Rebbell, and if it might be done with justice, the safest course were to take of his heade' (*Narration* p.76). Docwra made up his mind to go in person to Dublin to have these and other matters out with the Lord Deputy.

In terms of human suffering, the cost of the war had been appalling. The expeditionary force of 4,000 infantry and 200 cavalry that had landed at the Foyle three years earlier was reduced by 1603 to only 1,000 foot and 50 horse. According to Docwra's reckoning these figures included almost 2,000 reinforcements. The Derry garrison lost over 5,000 men killed, wounded or deserted[56]. Heavy military casualties give some indication of the numbers of civilians killed. Mountjoy's scorched-earth policy – 'frightfulness', as it was termed – of deliberately induced famine and often wholesale murder left much of Ulster a wasteland. Sir Arthur Chichester's most recent biographer explains how the troops under his command pursued a 'systematic campaign of starvation'.[57]

Mountjoy's secretary, Fynes Moryson, reported how even so ruthless a soldier as his commander could be moved when confronted with the consequences of his orders. Raiding towards Newry, Chichester and other officers

> felt a great savour, as it were roasting or broiling of flesh; the governor sent out the soldiers to search the wood, and they found a cabin where a woman was dead, a most horrible Spectacle of three Children (whereof the eldest was not above ten Years old,) all eating and gnawing with their Teeth the Entrails of their Mother, upon whose Flesh they had fed 20 Days past, and having eaten all from the Feet upward to the bare Bones, roasting it continually by a slow Fire, were now come to the eating of her said Entrails in like sort roasted, yet not divided from the Body, being as yet raw. The governor went to the place to see it, and demanded of them why they did so: they answered they could not get any other meat. It was demanded where their cows were, and they said the Englishmen had taken them way.[58]

Uncharacteristically, given his reputation, Chichester took pity on the children and ordered his troops to share their rations with them.

Moryson reported in 1602 how the common people were reduced

to eating nettles and docks, as evidenced by the numbers of them seen dead with their mouths coloured green. In July 1602 Lord Deputy Mountjoy reported with satisfaction to the Privy Council that 'we have none left to give us opposition, nor of late have seen any but dead carcasses, merely starved for want of meat, of which kind we found many in divers places as we passed'.[59] Troops under Docwra's command played a role in this butchery, and his *Narration* is replete with instances of wholesale slaughter of civilians. Killing non-combatants was a commonly accepted practice in early modern warfare. In the Nine Years War it became part of strategy.[60] The war forced the debasement of the coinage and cost the English exchequer two million pounds: an enormous amount by contemporary standards. Significantly, as Steven Ellis has pointed out, the eventual settlement 'hardly differed from what Tyrone had sought in 1594'.[61]

The end of the war brought a peace of sorts to Ulster. But there were many who feared the consequences of peace, especially those Irish who had fought alongside the English. In the aftermath of the war all victorious parties expected considerable reward from a grateful crown, but very few were satisfied. Those who gained most were the officers of the army in Ireland, even if many received less than they expected in the way of lands and pay.

The greatest losers of all were the Irish, particularly those who had assisted the English. At the very least they expected crown protection for their lives, liberty and lands. But, as far as the new king and his ministers were concerned, enough blood and treasure had been spilt in Ireland and it was evident that government policy would be to settle the kingdom as quickly as possible with the least expense. The cheapest solution was to restore Ó Néill and Ó Domhnaill to their lands and titles. The end of the war also brought an entirely new political situation, and a new set of courtiers around a new king. What little influence Docwra previously had as commander of a strategically vital garrison was now greatly dissipated. When Sir Henry resolved to go to Dublin in the spring of 1603 to discuss the settlement of Ulster with the Lord Deputy, uppermost in his mind of course were his own ambitions and a determination to obtain a satisfactory settlement of his account. Also on his agenda were the concerns of those Irish who had come to beg him to plead protection from the Lord Deputy against the now restored Earls of Tyrone and Tyrconnel. The Ó Catháin complained that Ó Néill had already 'sent some Men of his to be Cessed vpon him, which did intimate as if he were made Lord of his Countrey, [which he] woundered at', since it ran contrary to his agreement with the Lord Deputy to protect him. Muintir Dhochartaigh had heard that Inch Island had been granted to an English officer contrary to their agreement with Docwra. Toirrdhealbhach Ó Néill, son of Sir Art, challenged Sir Henry to fulfil his bargain to pass his father's lands into his ownership. Docwra had one other particular concern – the fate of 'My Guides & spyes, such as I had made many vses of, that the warres nowe ended, they might be restored to the landes they had formerlie dwelt vpon, & be saved from the Mallice of my lord of Tyrone & others that bore them a deadly hatred, onelie for the seruice they had done unto us'[62] (*Narration* p.75).

Moreover, the tortured affair of Niall Garbh had yet to be resolved. When they met at Dublin Castle, Docwra found the Lord Deputy '(as I thought) exceeding favourable, and well affected towards Mee'. The first item of business was the trial of Niall Garbh, and it was mutually agreed that Sir Henry should draw up the charges against him. As soon as attention turned to the settlement in Ulster, however, Mountjoy's announcement that Ó Néill was restored as earl and that Muintir Chatháin must show him obedience astonished Docwra. Reminding the Lord Deputy of his agreement with Ó Catháin and others, he bluntly asked, 'how I shall looke this man in the face when I shall knowe myselfe guilty directlie to haue falsified my word with him'. In reply Docwra was offered a lesson in politics. 'We must haue a Care to the Publique good,' Mountjoy reprimanded him, 'and giue Contentment to my lord of Tyrone, vpon which depends the Peace and securitie of the whole kingdome' (*Narration* p.77).

On the matter of young Toirrdhealbhach Ó Néill, Mountjoy asked Docwra to relay his promise to speak to the Earl of Tyrone in his favour. When Docwra protested, the Lord Deputy dramatically introduced Ó Néill in person to 'promise freelie to forgiue all that was past & to deal with them as kindlie as with the rest of his Tenants'. Shocked by the appearance in the Lord Deputy's chambers of an enemy he had spent years trying to bring to book, Docwra could only say of this promise that 'afterwardes I could giue particuler instance wherein he changed his Note and Sunge annother tune' (*Narration* p.79). When Docwra complained that the Earl of Tyrone had already summarily hanged one of his guides, he was peremptorily reminded that the earl was at liberty to exercise martial law. Docwra protested, 'but seeing the Bussines soe displeasing to my lord I gaue it ouer' (*Narration* p.79).

Sir Henry received more bad news on his own matters. He was ordered to hand back the fisheries of the Foyle which he had been promised as part of his reward for service, Mountjoy promising that 'yow shall be otherwise worthylie rewarded', and that he would press his case at court (*Narration* p.81).

In the end Docwra was left in no doubt about his subordinate position, and essentially told to carry out his orders without questioning the wisdom of government policy. Recalling these events over ten years later, he was still bitter. Even before he left Dublin, Sir Catháir Ó Dochartaigh presented him with conclusive evidence that, contrary to what he had been told by Mountjoy, Inch Island had been taken from them. Docwra set out for Derry in the company of the Earl of Tyrone's eldest son, Aodh, anxiously wondering how he could explain this policy to men who had fought alongside him, with whom he had brokered agreements, and who would now be delivered into the hands of their former masters. When the Ó Catháin was summoned to meet Docwra and the young Ó Néill lord at Derry, he was left in no position to debate terms although he protested that 'he followed my lord of Tyrone's Councell though it were against the kinge, seeing he was in this manner forced to be vnder him; In the end seeing noe remedie, hee shaked handes with my lord Hugh, bad "the devil take all English Men & as many as put theire trust in them"' (*Narration* p.81).

Sir Henry felt aggrieved that his reward, in his own estimation, did not meet his expectations for a generous settlement of his own affairs. He was now almost 40 years of age and evidently looked forward to a comfortable retirement after long hard years serving in the wars on the continent and in Ireland.[63] He had lost out financially because of the expediency of settling with Ó Néill, the man he had risked his life to bring to justice. Although he was made provost of the new town he lost some of the most lucrative royal licences such as the fisheries of the Foyle, remarking bitterly: 'here is the Reward I haue had to this day for my 21 yeares' seruice in the Warres before, my aucthoritie & Countenance one halfe diminished, the fishing of Loughfoyle taken away, & the land reserued from O'Caine' (*Narration* p.82). The villain of the piece in Sir Henry's account, apart from Aodh Ó Néill, is in fact the Irish administration. According to Docwra, they betrayed not only their own officers but also the Irish, without whose assistance the defeat of Ó Néill would have been a much lengthier, costlier and bloodier business.

Docwra was disappointed not only because by his own reckoning he had been sold short: by the lights of his day he was an honourable man and his word to the Irish had also been broken for political expediency. He was at heart a professional soldier, well aware of his inability to play the political game of flattery and manipulation: 'Artificiall or flourishing wordes to insinuate my selfe into favour by, I neither affect, nor Nature hath bestowed the giuft [gift] on Mee to use; But I professe to have a true faithfull Hearte, and yet, if the Course of my life have at any time told the Contrary, my Profession is vaine, and I have done, lett noe man beleeve Mee.' (*Narration* p.88)

Although he was made Governor of Lough Foyle and Provost of Derry, Docwra was determined to gain what he felt was his due and he left for England to press his own case at court. Once incident in particular, however, made him realise how matters had changed under the new administration. At an interview with Secretary of State Windebank, whose good offices he had previously relied on, Windebank answered his queries brusquely, then turned his back on him. The incident clearly rankled even a decade later, and Sir Henry recalled that 'There was nothing could fall unto Mee so farre beyond expectation, as this strange and soddaine [sudden] alienation of his Countenance from Mee.' (*Narration* p.82)

Finding no better satisfaction from other patrons, after six months he returned to Derry. He was not long back when he realised that news of discountenance at court preceded him and his status and authority were undermined by malicious rumour. He spent a year or more at Derry trying to make a fist of things, but recalled that

> from that day forward the people amongst whome I had before as much love as I thinke, as much respect I ame sure, as any man of my rancke [rank] in the Kingdome, beganne to Contemne [condemn] mee with as many Skornes [scorns] and affrontes, as the witt and malice of any that hated Mee could desire, or listed [wished] to putt into theire heades to doe Mee. (*Narration* p.83)

In the end, 'tyred with the exercise of Pacience ... dispareing of my safetie to live any longer in place', he returned to England, and 'resolved through with a greate deale of greife of minde and apparent loss of all my former laboures, to quitt myselfe of Ireland, and retourne noe more unto it', he sold his house and lands and the command of his soldiers to Sir George Paulet. He left Derry in 1608 and returned to England.

It may be argued that Docwra's dissatisfaction at his reward and his protestations of political naivety were somewhat disingenuous given that he went on to have a long and remunerative career as a civil servant in the Irish administration, holding many pensionable offices.[64] It may be in fact that he expected much more than he deserved. He was given licence to hold markets and a fair at Derry in 1603 and appointed as provost for life in July 1604 with the substantial pension of 20 shillings per diem.[65] He applied unsuccessfully for the Lord Presidency of Ulster in 1606, but was appointed instead a member for the Commission for Irish Causes.

Nonetheless, it is surely significant that most of his rewards came belatedly. He returned to Ireland in 1616 as Treasurer at War.[66] In 1624 he was appointed Keeper of the Peace in Leinster and Ulster, but it was almost 20 years after the defeat of Ó Néill before he was erected to the peerage and created Baron of Culmore in 1621. In 1627, when he was almost 60, he was appointed Keeper of the Great Seal of Ireland. Although he doubtless performed his tasks efficiently, he was never one of the leading lights of the administration and becomes historiographically almost invisible after the end of the Nine Years War. Perhaps the greatest compliment offered him, which as a soldier he may have appreciated most, came from the Irish themselves, who referred to Docwra as 'a distinguished knight of wisdom and ingenuity and a pillar of battle and valour'.[67]

Whatever cause for complaint Docwra had at the post-war settlement, he fared immeasurably better than his erstwhile Irish allies and enemies. Defeat eventually forced the Irish lords into exile on the continent, and the Flight of the Earls from Rathmullan in September 1607 was clearly an indirect or even a direct result of these events. The Great Earl of Tyrone died an exile at Rome in July 1616, 'seized with a settled melancholy'.[68] Aodh Ruadh Ó Domhnaill was already dead, allegedly poisoned by English agents during his embassy to Spain in 1602. In 1608 Docwra's young champion at Augher, Sir Catháir Ó Dochartaigh, was killed in desperate rebellion at Kilmacrenan in Donegal, after he had seized and burnt Derry, killing the governor –

the incompetent and arrogant Sir George Paulet. Ó Dochartaigh's sev-
ered head was displayed on the gates of Dublin. Paulet had managed
to undo in months Docwra's work of the previous years and to pro-
voke Muintir Dhochartaigh into rebellion. Sir Arthur Chichester's
biographer is clearly correct in pointing out the irony that had
Docwra remained at Derry, there is every likelihood that this rebellion
would never have occurred. In his departure there is also a certain
irony. Docwra, like so many fellow-officers, had been appalled when
a plantation did not materialise in the aftermath of the Nine Years
War … 'but [his] departure gave rise in no small measure to the
sequence of events which resulted in the enlargement of the Ulster
plantation'.[69]

Niall Garbh Ó Domhnaill also paid dearly. His wife Nuala, sister to
Aodh Ruadh, abandoned him for his treachery. The earldom and
lands of Tyrconnel that he so coveted were mostly granted by the
crown to the more pliable Rudhraighe Ó Domhnaill, and a warrant
issued for Niall Garbh's arrest on presumption of treason. In the light
of all that had happened in the intervening period, Sir Henry's opinions had mellowed even with regard to his most troublesome ally. In
the end, Docwra concluded sadly that

> there were noe vices in poore Neale Garvie … I Confess it made mee
> see cleere myne owne Errour, and the wronge (I may call it) I had
> done to Neale Garvye; [*Narration* p.86] not that my Conscience
> accuseth mee to have done any thinge towards him with malitious or
> corrupt intentions (noe whereof I take God to witnes my heart is
> cleere) But that with Simplicitie I sufferred my selfe to be made an
> Instrument of his overthrowe, under the pretence of those misbe-
> heavors, that were plainlie tollerated yea and allowed of in another,
> ffor it is true my lord [Mountjoy] would heare noe Complainte of
> him [Aodh Ó Néill] howe iust [just] soever.

At the time Docwra was writing his *Narration*, Niall Garbh Ó
Domhnaill was languishing in the Tower of London.[70] He had been
lodged there with Ó Catháin in 1608 after a jury failed to convict him
of treason.[71] Both men died in prison.

Sir Henry Docwra died in 1631, aged 67, after a long, if unremark-
able, second career as a civil servant. He is buried in Christchurch
Cathedral, Dublin.[72] For his own part, the *Narration* reveals that he
was proud of his military achievements but especially proud of the

'towne I had built at the Derrey'. He had every reason to take pride in his work. The charter of 1604 acknowledges his most enduring legacy:

> Sir Henry Docwra, Knt. in the reigns of Queen Elizabeth and King James, having, by his extraordinary valour, industry and charge, repossessed, repaired, repeopled, that town, being utterly ruinated, and laid waste, by the late rebellion in those parts. And having begun, and laid a good foundation there for the planting of a colony of civil and obedient people in that place, the king (for better progress therein, and the more fully establishing of the same in perpetuity, and for a memorial and recompence of the good service and charge which Sir Henry Docwra had employed and bestowed as aforesaid;) did pursuant to letters dated at Westminster 22nd March, 1603, give, grant, and confirm unto him and the inhabitants of the Derrie, and all the circuit and extent of land and water within the compass of three miles, to be measured from the circumference of the old church walls directly forth in a right line, every way round about, every mile containing 1000 geometrical paces, and every pace five feet in length, entire, and perfect City and County of itself to be called the City and County of Derrie, and shall be a Corporation and body politic ... Sir Henry to be Provost for life ...[73]

The establishment of a garrison city at Derry gave some measure of protection and confidence to the new settlers who arrived during the plantation. In this sense Docwra's campaign was a prerequisite for the Plantation of Ulster itself. Above all, it resulted eventually in the construction of the city of Londonderry, the cornerstone of English power in west Ulster. After Docwra, the English stayed.

1 It was reported to England in April that the Irish were busily raising defences on Lough Foyle and detaining those locals whose loyalty was doubtful (Sir Geoffrey Fenton to Sir Robert Cecil, 1 April, *Calendar of State Papers, Ireland, Elizabeth I, 1600* (London, 1903), p. 68; Fenton to Cecil, 8 April, ibid., p. 82. The English expected to be opposed by up to 5,000 foot and musketeers, 2,000 light troops, 1,000 pikemen and 900 cavalry, A scheme to disconcert the designs of the archtraitor Tyrone in the landing of the army at Lough Foyle, 12 March 1599, *Salisbury MSS*, vol. IX, pp. 99–102.

2 Compare, for example, the Ford of the Biscuits, 1594; Clontibret, 1595; Yellow Ford, 1598.

3 The war was also a three-kingdom conflict involving troops from England, Ireland, Scotland and Wales. 'Your lordships write of a Scottish gentleman that offereth himself to this service with 150 men, upon conditions in my opinion so reasonable, as I see no cause of refusal. He may undoubtedly be employed to singular good purpose in many respects, and specially for a mean of true intelligence, in which kind their nation are far more fit to use than any other, many of them being already dispersed all over the country and the truth of the Irish advertisements much to be measured by the concurrence with their reports' (Sir Henry Docwra to the Privy Council, 1 October 1600, *Calendar of State Papers, Ireland* (London, 1903), pp. 454–6, 457). Plans were also made to use the McCleans, traditional enemies of Cenél nEoghain, to harass the Irish in north Ulster (Lords of the Council to Mr Nicholson, 5 November 1600, *Historical Manuscripts Commission, Salisbury MSS*, vol. X, London, 1904, pp. 375–7). The Scots obviously had long-standing interests in Ulster, and on at least one occasion James VI intervened on behalf of Scottish merchants (King James VI to Sir Harry Dokray, 1 September 1600, *HMC Salisbury MSS*, vol. X, p. 377). I am indebted to Hiram Morgan for pointing out to me, among other things, that nothing ever came of plans to use Scottish troops and that the English did not want the Scots, Highlanders or Lowlanders, in Ulster.

4 Sir John Chamberlain to Dudley Carleton, 31 May 1598 (*Calendar of State Papers, Domestic, 1598–1601* (London, 1869), p. 57); Sir Henry Docwra to the Earl of Essex, Flushing, 25 January 1599 (*HMC Salisbury MSS*, vol. IX (London, 1902), pp. 41–2).

5 *Calendar of State Papers, Ireland, 1599–1600*, p. 160.

6 'A relation of the manner of government of the kingdom of Ireland as the Earl of Essex left it …' (30 September 1599, *Calendar of State Papers, Ireland, 1599–1600*, p. 160). Shortly before he went to Ireland in April Essex wrote to the Privy Council in England telling him that he had heard from Docwra 'how ill Her Majesty's Army is cared for in Ireland and how miserable I am like to find it' (*Calendar of State Papers, Ireland, 1599–1600*, p. 1).

7 Privy Council Motions, 9 January 1600, *Calendar of State Papers, Ireland, 1599–1600*, p. 393.

8 Falls, C., *Elizabeth's Irish Wars* (London, 1950), p. 96; Hayes-McCoy, op. cit., p. 86.

9 According to the English the explosion was accidental, caused by an outbreak of fire near the powder. According to the Irish the incident was providential, caused by a wolf carrying a firebrand in its mouth, a punishment on the invaders for desecrating the monastery of St Colm Cille. The terrified English soldiers ran from their lodgings in the Teampull Mór screaming that the great Irish god, Columba, 'has killed us all'. See, Simpson, R., *The Annals of Derry*, reprint (Limavady, 1987), pp. 19–21,; Milligan, C.D., *The Walls of Derry*, reprint, pp. 6–7 (Armagh, 1986). It is worth remarking here that while Colmcille is

generally regarded as the founder of early Derry, Sir Henry Docwra might be regarded as the founder of the early modern city.

10  For a fuller account of the strategy involved, see Ellis, S.G., *Tudor Ireland* (London, 1985), pp. 308–9 and Falls, op. cit., pp. 241, 244 and *passim*. For an outline of the plan see 'A scheme to disconcert the designs of the archtraitor Tyrone in the landing of the army at Lough Foyle', 12 March 1599, *HMC Salisbury MSS*. I am indebted to John McGurk for pointing out that the pincer strategy was anticipated by Francis Jobson, Surveyor in Sir William Fitzwilliam's administration in 1591. He sent in a map with a tract entitled 'Ulster's Unity'. The tract, a coloured plot, shows garrisons at Coleraine, Newry, Strabane and Belfast, but not Derry. See PROMPF, 312.

11  Cyril Falls credits Essex with developing this strategy: see, Falls, C., *Mountjoy: Elizabethan General* (London, 1955), p. 241. However, Docwra was one of the officers who advocated the strategy (see 'The opinion of the Lords and Colonels of the Army, dissuading the journey northward', *Calendar of State Papers, Ireland, 1599–1600*, 21 August 1599, pp. 126–7; Mullin, T.H. & Mullan, J.E., *The Ulster Clans* (Belfast, 1966), p. 77.

12  'A scheme to disconcert the designs of the archtraitor Tyrone in the landing of the army at Lough Foyle', 12 March 1599, *HMS Salisbury MSS*, IX, pp. 99–102.

13  The best account of Docwra's strategy is his letters to the Privy Council soon after his arrival. He advocated killing all the cattle and burning the corn as the most efficacious means of ending the war (see Sir Henry Docwra to the Privy Council, 24 May 1600, *Calendar of State Papers, Ireland*, pp. 194–198, p. 195). The best account of contemporary warfare can be found in McGurk, J., *Elizabethan Conquest*, chapter 9, pp. 220–39.

14  Docwra's orders from the Privy Council specifically enjoined him to 'hold a discreet and temperate course to draw in so many of the better sort of Irish as you can ... to use faithful instruments and if need be to send them amongst the Irish to labour and work them' (see *Narration*).

15  This plan had originally been suggested by the ill-fated Earl of Essex, executed in February 1601 after a failed *coup d'état* partly prompted by his fall from royal favour over his disastrous performance in Ireland (see Mullin & Mullan, op. cit., p. 77; Milligan, op. cit., p. 8).

16  Sir Henry Docwra to the Privy Council, Derry, 24 May 1600, *Calendar of State Papers, Ireland, 1600*, p. 194; Captain Humphrey Willis to Symon Willis, Derry, 25 May 1600, ibid., pp. 199–202, p. 201.

17  The lack of resistance is readily accounted for. To give Docwra time to land and establish a fort, Mountjoy attacked in south-east Ulster to draw off the Irish forces (see Sir Geoffrey Fenton to Cecil, 8 April 1600, *Calendar of State Papers, Ireland*, p. 82).

18  The best modern accounts of Derry in this period are Lacy, B., *Siege City, the Story of Derry and Londonderry* (Belfast, 1990), pp. 72–6; Mullin, T.H., *Ulster's Historic City* (Coleraine, 1986), pp. 12–21; Milligan, op. cit., pp. 6–13.

19  The abbey was the Dubh-Regles or Black Church, and the two churches St. Augustine's and the Templemore.

20  Lacy, op. cit., p. 74. One of Docwra's officers described how 'the Derrey ... a place sweetly situated' could readily be made an island by cutting a trench from the bog to the river (Sir William Windsor to the Earl of Essex, 8 July 1600, *HMC Salisbury MSS*, vol. X (London, 1904), pp. 225–7.

21  Mullin, op. cit., p. 79.

22  Docwra to the Privy Council, 24 May 1600, *Calendar of State Papers, Ireland, 1600*, pp. 194–98. On Docwra's care for his men, see McGurk, J., 'Casualties

and welfare measures for the sick and wounded of the Nine Years War in Ireland, 1594–1603', *Journal of the Society for Army Historical Research*, 1990, vol. 68, pp. 22–35 and 188–204.

23  Privy Council Motions, 9 January 1600, *Calendar of State Papers, Ireland, 1599–1600*, p. 393. Their religious well-being was fostered by a preacher appointed for this task.

24  The *Annals of the Four Masters* reported that the incident occurred when the English tried to recover a large number of horses taken by Ó Domhnaill: 'One of Ó Domhnaill's kinsmen, namely, Aodh, the son of Aodh Duv, son of Aodh Roe, made a well aimed cast of a javelin at the General, Sir Henry Docwra, and, striking him directly in the forehead, wounded him very severely' (*The Annals of the Kingdom of Ireland by the Four Masters*, John O'Donovan (ed.), 2nd edn (Dublin, 1856), vol. VI, p. 2209).

25  Earl of Ormonde to the Lord Deputy, Kilkenny, 15 August 1600; *Calendar of State Papers, Ireland*, p. 357.

26  Arrangements were hastily made at London to ship more beer to Derry; *Calendar of State Papers, Ireland*, p. 403. The *Annals of the Four Masters* (p. 2193) describes how the garrison 'were seized with distemper and disease, on account of the narrowness of the place which they were, and the heat of the summer season. Great numbers of them died of this sickness.'

27  Docwra to the Privy Council, 27 August 1600, *Calendar of State Papers, Ireland*, p. 380.

28  Docwra to the Privy Council, 2 September 1600, *Calendar of State Papers, Ireland*, p. 406.

29  The Irish gave deserters free passage, food and shelter throughout their territories. The men were then shipped to Scotland and thence home. According to one English officer the Welsh and Lancashire men were the worst offenders (Captain Humphrey Willis to Secretary Cecil, Dublin, 24 January 1601, *Calendar of State Papers, Ireland*, p. 161). John McGurk has pointed out to me that not all these deserters returned to England or Wales; some served instead with the Irish forces.

30  Docwra to the Privy Council, 2 September 1600, *Calendar of State Papers, Ireland*, pp. 407–8. Coolmackatrene (Coolmacatraine) has been known since the nineteenth century as Castleforward (see *Letters containing information relative to the Antiquities of the County of Donegal collected during the progress of the Ordnance Survey in 1835*, reproduced under the direction of the Rev. Michael O'Flanagan (Bray, 1927), p. 78.

31  Sir Geoffrey Fenton to Secretary Cecil, Dublin, 27 October 1600, *Calendar of State Papers, Ireland, 1600*, pp. 520–22.

32  'There he procured Sir John to be of his faction, and so they both stood out upon their guard in a neutrality betwixt our forces and O'Donnell. And in this interim they surprised Strabane, carried away all the pillage and quit the pile ... and then Neale Garve went and took the Lifford' (Sir Geoffrey Fenton to Secretary Cecil, 27 October 1600, *Calendar of State Papers, Ireland, 1600*, p. 520; Docwra to Cecil, 2 November 1600, *Calendar of State Papers, Ireland, 1600–1601*, p. 13).

33  Ibid. According to one English source, when Aodh Ó Néill learned of Niall Garbh's treachery 'he was so dumb-stricken, that he did not eat nor drink in three days and soon after requested a parley' (Captain Humphrey Willis to Cecil, 29 October, *Calendar of State Papers, Ireland, 1600*, p. 535. Niall Garbh was described by one Irish commentator as having 'combined the venom of the asp with the daring of a lion'.

34 *Calendar of State Papers, Ireland, 1600–1601*, introduction, p. xvi.

35 The Clann Daibhéid had fostered Cathaír Ó Dochartaigh and were outraged at the preference given to his uncle. For a fuller account of these events see Meehan, C.P., *The Fate and Fortunes of the Earl of Tyrone and Rory O'Donel, Earl of Tyrconnel* (Dublin, 1868), pp. 292–5.

36 Fenton to Cecil, 8 April 1600, *Calendar of State Papers, Ireland*, p. 82.

37 Sir Henry Docwra to the Privy Council, Carrickfergus, 11 May 1600; *Calendar of State Papers, Ireland*, pp. 173–4. Docwra's only intelligence on landing, his spies having ominously not returned to camp, was from Sir Art Ó Néill; *Calendar of State Papers, Ireland*, p. 194, 24 May. Sir John Doherty (Seán Ó Dochartaigh) would probably have defected immediately had it not been for Aodh Buidhe, 'a creature of O'Donnell's' (Docwra to the Privy Council, 24 May 1600, *Calendar of State Papers, Ireland*, pp. 194–8).

38 The importance of the divisions among the Irish in assisting the English was very evident to the Four Masters, who lamented: 'Wo is me that these heroes of Kinel-Connell were not united in fight on one side against their enemies, and that they were not at peace; for, while they remained so, they were not banished or driven from their native territories, as they afterwards were!' (*Annals of the Four Masters*, p. 2217).

39 Sir Henry Docwra to the Privy Council, 2 July 1601 (*Calendar of State Papers, Ireland, 1600–1601*, pp. 410–413).

40 Privy Council to Sir Henry Docwra, Richmond, 5 November 1600 (*Calendar of State Papers, Ireland, 1600–1601*, p. 18).

41 *Annals of the Four Masters*, p. 2213.

42 Docwra to Cecil, 2 November 1600 (*Calendar of State Papers, Ireland*, p. 13).

43 Falls, *Elizabeth's Irish Wars*, p. 272.

44 Compare Docwra's comments at the death of Sir Art Ó Néill in late November with his estimation of Muintir Dhochartaigh. Sir Art had in fact fought along-side the English almost since the first day they landed. According to Sir Henry he died of a surfeit of alcohol during the celebration of his recent marriage: 'Sir Art O'Neill is dead of drinking too many carouses upon his marriage day. There is no great loss of him, a very dull fellow, nor McSwyne's being turned traitor.' Earlier letters to the Council reveal that Sir Art may in fact have died from the fever raging in the English camp compounded by the twin exertions of his nup-tials and an addiction to drink.

45 Sir John Bolles to Cecil, 7 March 1601 (*Calendar of State Papers, Ireland* , pp. 205–7). The bishop's death was also reported as having occurred when the Derry garrison captured a church and put to the sword 'the Prior of Derry and twenty of the principal priests in all Ulster'. Extract of a letter to Lord Deputy Mountjoy, Drogheda, 12 March 1601, forwarded to Cecil, 31 March (*Calendar of State Papers, Ireland*, pp. 247–8).

46 The Derry garrison was resupplied with sufficient match by Sir Arthur Chichester in early August.

47 Docwra to the Privy Council, 10 August 1601 (*Calendar of State Papers, Ireland, 1601–1603*, pp. 20–21).

48 G. Lord Hunsden to Robert Cecil, 7 June 1601: 'I return to you the large and painful reports of Sir Har. Dokerie's plots and journeys, which no ways alter my former opinion conceived of him, that he never intended to shorten the wars, but with some good few words give a taste of his willingness; yet in the end his performances fall short of his promises' (*HMC Salisbury MSS*, vol. XI, pp. 219–20).

49 See, for instance, Cecil's recommendation of Covert to command a company at

Derry, Lord Deputy Mountjoy and some of the Council to the Privy Council, camp before Newry, 28 October 1600 (*Calendar of State Papers, Ireland, 1600*, p. 524); Mountjoy to Cecil, 27 October 1600 (ibid., p. 517); Covert informed Cecil that when he attempted to carry out his duties in checking the musters he was 'daily ... boldly threatened to have our throats cut' (Falls, *Elizabeth's Irish Wars*, p. 275).

50 'An answer to certain questions made by the Right Honourable the Lord Treasurer and Mr Secretary [Cecil] and some other of the Council concerning Sir Henry Dock[wra's] government at Lough Foyle' (*Calendar of State Papers, Ireland, 1600–1601*, pp. 111–13).

51 Secretary Cecil to Sir John Bolles, 10 September 1600 (*Calendar of State Papers, Ireland, 1600*, pp. 416–18); see also Bolles to Cecil, 13 October 1601 (*HMC Salisbury MSS*, vol. XI, p. 425): 'I beseech you either to grant my long suit to be freed from that service, or that at least I may be employed where Sir Henry Docwra may not command me.'

52 Secretary Cecil to Sir John Bolles (ibid.); see also *Calendar of State Papers, Ireland, 1600*, pp. 416, 418, 457.

53 Docwra remarked that he could never discover whether the destruction was by accident or design.

54 Docwra remembered the date as 24 March, which was in fact the date of the death of Elizabeth I – an event deliberately kept from Tyrone by Lord Mountjoy, who feared that he would hold out for better terms from the new king.

55 It is worth reproducing here Sir Henry's pen portrait of Niall Garbh in defence of the charge that the Irish had deceived him: 'For Neill Garve I cannot compare him to anything more like a quince. Let him be sugared and dressed with much cost and he will be good for somewhat, but undoubtedly, to speak truth of the man, I am of the opinion that the Queen must of necessity bestow more upon him than his body is worth before she shall reap any good of his service; although the man is valiant, of reasonable account in the country among some men of quality, and in the taking of Lifford only did a singular good piece of service, and may do much more, being tempered and kept in subjection according to the quality of his unbridled nature, which is apparently prone to tyranny where he may command, to proud and importunate beggary where he is subject, to extreme covetousness whether he be rich or poor, and unseasoned by any manner of discipline, knowledge, or fear of God.' (Note by Sir Henry Docwra, March 1602, *Calendar of State Papers, Ireland*, pp. 259–64, p. 263; cited in Falls, *Elizabeth's Irish Wars*, p. 271.)

56 Some troops were also transferred to other commands.

57 'It would be simplistic to argue that the present-day sparsity of catholics in south Antrim and north Down should be entirely attributed to his systematic campaign of starvation; but that he made a major contribution to the present religio-political configuration of these areas cannot be precluded.' (McCavitt, J., *Sir Arthur Chichester, Lord Deputy of Ireland, 1605–1616* (Belfast, 1998), p. 13.)

58 McCavitt, ibid.

59 Mullin & Mullan, op. cit., p. 90; Bardon,, J., *History of Ulster* (Belfast, 1992), p. 113.

60 Pocock, J.G.A., 'The Atlantic Archipelago and the War of the Three Kingdoms', citing Morgan, H., *Tyrone's rebellion: the outbreak of the Nine Years War in Tudor Ireland*, in Morrill, J. & Bradshaw, B. (eds), *The British Problem* (London, 1996), p. 175. Morgan asserts little difference between the queen's men and the chiefs, 'the men of law and the men of the sword, behave in ways in which there is singularly little to choose'. Pocock, quite rightly, contrasts Jenny Wormwald's

view that although the levels of violence were undoubtedly high in blood-feud societies they were nevertheless containable, 'whereas in societies governed by king and law the level of public violence is occasionally explosive and devastating' Wormwald, J., 'Bloodfeud , kindred and government in early modern Scotland', *Past and Present*, vol. LXXX (1980), pp. 54–97. Docwra's *Narration* makes clear that the levels of violence visited on the population by English troops in Ulster were unprecedented in terms of casualties.

61 Ellis, S.G., *Tudor Ireland*, pp. 311–12; For an alternative reading see Morgan (op. cit.), who points out that the land-holding situation was the same as before but otherwise the situation had altered completely in that the country was now conquered and dotted with English garrisons.

62 The son of one of these spies had told Docwra that the earl of Tyrone had already hanged his father.

63 Docwra's year of birth is variously given as 1560, 1563 or 1568. See *Dictionary of National Biography*, vol. XXV, p. 141.

64 There is evidence that Docwra had made enemies by his own duplicity rather than political naivety. See, for example, Christopher Sacheverell to the Earl of Essex, 1599, wherein he complains that 'by sinister practices' Docwra had managed to have his office passed to Sir George Cary to the petitioner's great disadvantage (*HMC Salisbury MSS*, vol. XIV, Addenda (London, 1923), p. 100; Paul Gwyn to the king, 1603, re Sir Henry Docwra who had drawn him to Ireland 'to his utter undoing', abused his name and owes him 579l. (ibid., p. 378).

65 *Patent Rolls, Ireland*, I, part I (1846), pp. 114–15.

66 Docwra was forced to defend his post on occasion (see Sir Henry Docwra to Viscount Villiers, Dublin, 9 November 1616, *HMC Fortescue MSS*, Report 2 (Dublin, 1874), p. 52).

67 *Annals of the Four Masters*, vol. VI, p. 2193.

68 *Dictionary of National Biography*, vol. XLI, p. 196.

69 McCavitt, op. cit., p. 142.

70 Niall Garbh's most eloquent advocate was in fact Sir Richard Hadsor, who appealed to Secretary Cecil directly on his behalf over Docwra's head (see Sir Richard Hadsor to Cecil, 23 June 1603, *HMC Salisbury MSS*, vol. XV (London, 1930), pp. 145–6.

71 For a brief account of these events see McCavitt, op. cit., pp. 145–7. For an argument that Niall Garbh had a case to answer see also Clarke, A., 'Pacification, plantation, and the catholic question, 1603–23', in the *New History of Ireland*, vol. III, pp. 187–232.

72 Crosthwaite, J.C. and Todd, J.H., *The Book of Obits and Martyrology, Christchurch* (Dublin, 1884), s.v. Docwra.

73 Reprinted in Simpson, *Annals of Derry* (reprint, Limavady, 1987), pp. 22–3.

# A NARRATION

*of the*

## SERVICES DONE BY THE ARMY YMPLOYED TO LOUGH-FOYLE

### VNDER THE LEADINGE OF MEE SR HENRY DOCWRA KNIGHT,

CHARLES LORD MOUNTIOY BEING THEN LORD DEPUTIE (AFTERWARDS EARLE OF DEUONSHIRE AND LORD LEWETENANT) OF IRELAND.

*togeather with*

# A DECLARATION

*of the*

## TRUE CAUSE & MANNER OF MY COMING AWAY AND LEAVING THAT PLACE,

*Written in the sommer 1614, & finished the first of September the same year.*

*[Copied from an old MS. At the Ordnance Survey Office, exhibiting on the fly leaf "Theo, Docwra," J. O'D.]*

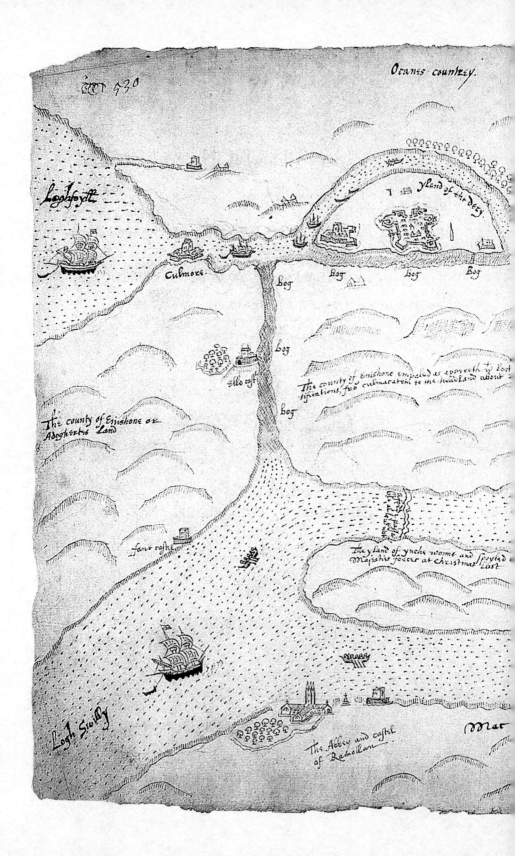

Ocanes countrey.

ꝯꝯꞇ 530

Loghfoytt

Culmore

Yland of the derry

bog

Bog

Bog

Bog

Allo oft

bog

bog

The county of Enishone empaled as apereth by fortifications fro culmare even to the headland about

The county of Enishone or Adoghertie Land

fane caftel

The yland of ynche worme and Maiesties forces at christmas spoyled loft

The Abbey and caftel of Ramollan

Logh Swilly

Mar

Streabane.

Oonalong.

fort

fort

Curgan

Bog

fort

fort

fort

Bog

fort

Bog

Bog

Lephard.

Tyreonel.

fort

Culmacatrem

Bog

The stronge castell of
Burt in possessio of Hubay

Here abowt men may wade
at low water to Burt castell

Logh Swilly.

Swynes cowntrey.

213

R. Ashby.

# A NARRATION

&c

THE occasion that moued mee, to make this Narration, was giuen by my lord Chichester, (the lord Deputie of Ireland that now is) who being in England some two or three monethes of this last Sommer, neere the time of his departure, when I came to take my leaue of him, pleased to enter into some speech with mee touching my Retyred Life, which hee imputed to proceed from my owne disposition, averring he often heard my Lord of Deuonshire say, that nothing would Content mee except I had all, & such a Commaund as might not stand with the convenience of the King's seruice; I made noe large replie vnto his Lordship then, because the time serued not for it; But somewhat I saide, to excuse myselfe from that imputation & withall it came round at that instant into my Remembraunce that I had (not long before) heard myselfe in like manner taxed for selling away of my place: soe as I found the two mayne Points the world misconceiued mee in, were these: ffirst that I voluntarily gaue ouer my Place, & then that I made a Benifitt thereof, by selling it away to an other, & if either of these were true, whatsoeuer ensued upon it, afterwards to my greife & discontentment, I cannot but acknowledge, I may iustlie be Convinced, the faulte was myowne, I haue noe Cause to Complaine: But for Refutation of those fewe obiections, as I said then to his Lordship in priuate, soe now I may safelie proclaime it to the world, I neede not appeale to any other Testimonye but that of his owne knowledge. Then coming home and falling into a sadd meditation with my Selfe, it came into my thoughts shall I for euer by silence betray myne owne Innocency, was it a vertue in a Dumbe Man, to breake the very tongue strings, to speake when he sawe his father in Danger, to be otherwise vniustlie Condemned, & can it be Excusable in mee, that Nature hath not denied the vse of my tongue vnto, to

41

suffer my Bowels to frett with greife, my Reputation to be trampled vpon, (which all men knowe ought to be deerer to Mee than my owne Life, & as deere as the redemption of my ffathers,) & so lett it pass, & say nothing? yea, but I speake alone (without Adversarie) may some man say, and if I faine any, it is such a one as is gone ex rerum Natura, against whome I may assume what libertie I will, so say what I list: it is true this may be obiected: but I have this to say againe, for these thinges I discourse of touching my owen particuler greevances, they are such as I openlie speak & Complayned of in his life time, & for the rest touching the carriage of the gennerall bussines, there are I thinke hundreds at least yet living able to Controwle mee if I speake vntruth, & whatsoever I say in either out of the Compase of comon Knowledge, I haue Evidence to shewe, for that any man shall see that will, and when he hath done lett him iudge as his owen Discretion shall guide him. And I say further, my desire is with truth to defend my selfe, not with mallice to defame the memorie of an other, & my lord was a Noble man that for many yeares togeather, I loued & honnored sincerelie in my hearte, vertues I sawe in him that moued mee soe to doe, they were not, nor could not be all extinguished by one acte, though of neuer soe manifest a wronge done vnto mee: Besides, it may be that somewhat there was, that reason in his apprehension might moue him vnto, the secret whereof it seamed not fitt in his Eyes to impart vnto mee: let it be soe, for that doth nothing infringe the truth of that I say, But entring into further discourse with myself touching this subiect, it came with all into my minde, I had lying by mee some memoriall noates and a greate Number of letters, that if they were well searched ouer, togeather with the helpe of myne owne memorie, were able to bring to light the truth of that which otherwise was like to perish and Consume in Darkenes: I spent a litle time to pervse them, & these are the effectes, the doing thereof hath produced.

The Army consisting in List of 4000 foote & 200 horse, whereof 3000 of the foote, & all the horse were levied in England, the other 1000 foote were taken of the old Companys about Dublin, & all assigned to meete att Knockfergus, the first of May: That part levyed in England was shipt at Helbree neere vnto westchester on the 24th of Aprill, 1600. And of these a Regiament of 1000 ffoote & 50 horse, were to be taken out immediatelie vpon our landing, & assigned to sr Mathew Morgan to make a plantation with att Ballishannon.

The Provisions wee carried with vs at first were a quantetie of deale Boards & Sparrs of ffirr timber, a 100 flock bedds, with other necessaries to furnish an Hospitall withall one Peece of Demy Cannon of Brass, two Culverins of Iron, a master Gunner, two master Masons, & two master Carpenters, allowed in pay with a greate number of Tooles & other vtensiles, & with all victuell & munition requisite.

Soe with those men from England, and with these Provisions aforesaide, on the xxv day of Aprill wee sett saile, and on the 28th in the Euening put in att Knockfergus, where wee staide the space of 8 dayes before the Companyes from Dublin came all vnto vs.

The last of them coming in by the 6th of May, on the 7th wee sett saile againe, & the windes often fayling, & sometimes full against vs, it was the 14th before wee could putt in to the mouth of the Bay at Loughfoyle, & noe sooner were wee entred, but wee fell on ground, & soe stucke till the next day, then at a full tide, wee waighed our Anchors, sayled a little way and rune on ground againe.

On the 16th in the morning wee gott loose, & about 10 of the Clocke (100 men lying on shoare, & giuing vs a volie of shott, & soe retyring,) wee landed att Culmore, & with the first of our horse & foote that wee could vnshipp, made vp towards a troupe of horse and foote, that wee sawe standing before vs on the topp of a hill, but by ignorance of the wayes our horses were presentlie boggt, & soe at that day wee made none other vse, but onlie to land our men. The next day, the place seaming to my Judgement fitt to build, wee begaune about the Butt end of the old broken Castle, to cast vp a fforte, such as might be capable to lodge 200 men in.

Six days wee spent in labour about it, in which meane space, making vpp into the Countrie with some troupes (onely with intent to discover,) wee came to Ellogh a castle of O'Doghartey's, which he had newlie abandoned & begunne to pull downe, Butt seeing it yett Tennable, & of good vse to be held, I put Captaine Ellis ffloudd into it, and his Companie of 150 men.

On the 22nd of May wee put the Army in order to marche, & leauing Captain Lancellott Atford at Culmore with 600 men, to make vp the workes, wee went to the Derry 4 myles of vpon the River side a place in manner of an Iland Comprehending within it 40 acres Ground, wherin were the Ruines of a old Abbay, of a Bishopp's house, of two Churches, & at one of the ends of it of an old Castle, the River called loughfoyle encompassing it all on one side, & a bogg most comonlie wett, & not easilie passable except in two or three places dividing it from the maine land.

This peece of Ground we possest our selves of without Resistaunce, & iudging it a fitt place to make our maine plantation in, being somewhat hie, & therefore dry, & healthie to dwell vpon, att that end where the old Castle stood, being Close to the water side, I pressentlie resolued to raise a fforte to keep our stoore of Munition & victuells in, & in the other a litle aboue, where the walls of an old Cathedrall church were yet standing, to evert annother for our future safetie & retreate vnto upon all occasions.

Soe then I vnloaded & discharged the Shipping that brought vs, all but those reserued for Sr. Math : Morgan & two Men of Warre, vnder comaund of Captaine George Thornton, & Captaine Thomas Fleminge, which were purposlie assigned to attend vs all that Sommer : & the first bussines I setled myselff vnto was, to lay out the forme of the said two intended ffortes, & to assigne to every Companye his severall taske how & where to worke.

I know there were some that presentlie beganne to censure mee, for not sturring abroade, & makeing iourneyes vp into the Countrye, alleadging wee were stronge enough & able to doe it; I deny not but wee were; but that was not the scope & drift of our coming, wee were to sitt it out all winter, Prayes would not be sett without many hazards, & a greate Consumption of our men, the Countrie was yet vnknowne vnto vs, & those wee had to deale with were, as I was sure, would Chuse or Refuse to feight with vs as they sawe theire owne advantage; These Considerations moued mee to resolue to hould an other Course, & before I attempted any thinge els, to setle & make sure the footing wee had gayned.

The two shipps of warre, therefore, (the Countrie all about vs being wast & burned,) I sent with souldiers in them to coast all alonge the shoare, for the space of 20 or 30 myles, & willed wheresoeuer they found any howses, they should bring a way the Timber & other materialls to build with all, such as they could; and O'Cane hauing a woode, lying right over against vs, (on the other side of the River,) wherein was plentie of old growne Birch, I daylie sent workemen with a Guard of souldiers to cutt it downe; & there was not a sticke of it brought home, but was first well fought for; A Quarrie of stone & slatt wee found hard at hand, Cockle shells to make a Lyme, wee discouered infinite plentie of, in a litle Iland in the mouth of the

Harbour as wee came in, and with those helpes, togeather with the Provisions wee brought, & the stones and rubbidge of the old Buildings wee found, wee sett ourselues wholie, & with all the dilligence wee could possible to fortefying & framing, & setting vpp of howses, such as wee might be able to liue in, & defend ourselves when winter should Come, & our men be decayed as it was apparent it would be : And whether this was the right Course to take or noe, let them that sawe the after Events be the Judges of.

My Lord Deputie, att the time wee should land, (to make our discent the more easie,) was drawne downe to the Blackwater, & gaue out that hee would enter the Countrey that way, whereupon Tyrone & O'Donell had assembled theire cheifest strength to oppose against him : But his lordship now knowing wee were safe on shore, & possest of the ground wee ment to inhabite, with drewe his Campe & retourned to Dublin, & then being deliuered of that feare, those forces they had brought togeather for that purpose, being now encreased by the addition of more, & estimated (by Comon fame) to be about 5000 in all, they came downe with vpon vs, & placing themselues in the night within litle more then a mile from where wee lay, earelie in the morning at the Breaking vpp of the watch, gaue on vpon our Corps de Guard of horse, chased them home to our foote Sentynells, & made a countennaunce as if they came to make but that one daye's worke of it but the Alarume taken, & our men in Armes, they contented themselves to attempe noe further, but seeking to drawe vs forth into the Countrey where they hoped to take vs at some advantages, & finding wee stoode vpon our defensiue onelie, after the greatest parte of the day spent in skirmish, a litle without our Campe they departed towards the Eueninge, whither did wee thinke it fitt to pursue them.

An now did Sr Mathew Morgan demand his Regiament of 1000 foote, and 50 horse, which at first (as I saide before) were designed him for a plantation att Ballyshannon; but vpon consultation held how hee should proceed, & with what Probabilitie he might be able to effect that intended bussines, there appeared soe many wants & difficulties vnthought on, or vnprouided; for before that it was euident those forces should be exposed to mainfest ruine, if at that time, & in the state as thinges then stoode, hee should goe forward, the truth whereof being Certified both by himselfe & mee to the lords of the Councell in England, as alsoe to the lord Deputie & Councell of

Ireland; wee receiued present directions from them both to suspend the proceeding in that action till annother time; & soe I discharged the Rest of the shipping reserued for the iourney; & not long after the Companys' growing weake, & the list of the foote reduced to the number of 3000, that Regiament was wholie dissolued & made as a parte onelie of our army.

On the first of June, Sr Arthur O'Neale, sonne to old Tirlogh Lenogh that had beene O'Neale, came in vnto mee with some 30 horse & foot, a Man I had directions from the state, to labour to drawe to our side, & to promise to be made Earle of Tyroane, if the other that mainteyned the Rebellion could be dispossessed of the Country; By his aduice with in fewe dayes after I sent Sr John Chamberlaine with 700 men into O'Cane's Countrie, to enter into it by boate, from O'Dohertye's side, because at the hither end lying right over against vs, was a Continuall watch kepte, soe as we could not stirre but wee were sure to be presentlie discouered; These men marching all night put ouer at Greene-castle, & by breake of day, on the 10th of June, fell in the middest of theire Creagtes vnexpected, Ceazed a greate pray, & brought it to the Waterside; but for want of meanes to bring it all away, they hackt & mangled as many as they could, & with Some 100 Cowes, which they put abord theire Boats, besids what the Souldiers brought away kild, they retourned.

On the 28th June, came some men of O'Dohertyes, & lay in ambush before Ellogh, the Garrison discouering them, fell out & skirmisht, a litle of from the Castle: wee perceiued them from the Derry to be in feight, I tooke 40 horse & 500 ffoote, and made towards them; when they sawe vs coming they left the skirmish & drewe away; wee followed up as fast as wee could, & coming to the foote of a mountaine, which they were to pass ouer in theire retreate, wee might see them all march before vs, though but slowlie, yet with as much speede as they were able to make, being, to our grieffe, about 400 foote, & 60 horse, & wee makeing as much hast on our partes to ouertake them: By that time the last of them had obtained the topp of the hill: Sr John Chamberlaine & I, with some 10 horse more, were come vpp close in theire heeles, all our foote & the rest of our horse coming after vs as fast as they could but all out of breath & exeedinglie tired; Hauing thus gained the very topp of the hill, & seeing but fewe about me I stayed & badd a stand to be made till more Company might come vpp, and withall casting my head about, to see how our men followed, I seeing the foote farr behinde, & our horse but slowlie Clyming vpp, twining about a gaine I might see sr John Chamberlaine vnhorsed, lying on the ground a stone's cast before mee, & at least a Dozen hewing at him with theire Swordes, I presentlie gaue forward to haue rescued him, & my horse was shott in two places & fell deade vnder mee, yet they forsooke him vpon it, & wee recouered his bodie, but wounded with 16 woundes, & instantlie giving vp the Ghost, wherevpon wee made a stand in the place, & staying till more Companie came vp, wee brought him off, & suffered them to march a way without further pursuite.

On the second of July I put 800 men into Boates & landed them att Dunalong. Tyrone (as we were tould) lying in Campe within two myles of the Place, where I presentlie fell to raiseing a Forte, his men came downe & skirmisht with vs all that day, but perceiuing the next, wee were tilted & out of hope to be ablt to remoue vs, they rise vp & left vs quietlie to doe what we would, where after I had made it reasonablie defensible, I left Sr John Bowles in Garrison with 6 Companyes of Foote, & afterwards sent him 50 horse.

On the 14th of July came O'Donnell with a troupe of 60 horse, & earely in the Morninge as our watch was ready to be discharged fell vpon a Corpes de Guard of some 20 of our horse, but they defended themselues without loss & orderlie retyred to the Quarter, only Captaine John Sidney was hurte in the shoulder with the blow of a staffe.

On the 29th of July he came againe with 600 Foote, & 60 Horse, & lay close in ambush in a valley within a quarter of a myle of our outmost horse sentinells, & Moyle Morrogh Mac Swyndoe (a man purposelie sent with mee by the state, & soe well esteemed of, as the queene had giuen a Pention of vi. s. a day vnto during his life, & the present Comaund of 100 English souldiers,) hauing intelligence with him, caused some of his men to goe a litle before Breake of Day, & driue forth our horses, (that were vsually euery night brought into the Iland to Graze) directlie towards him, In soe much as vpon the sodaine before any thinge could be done to preuent it, he gott to the number of 60 [160?] into his power, & presentlie made hast to be gone. By the alarum, I rise vp from my Bedd, tooke some 20 horses, & such foote as were readie, Bidd the rest follow, & soe made after them. At fower myles end wee ouertooke them, theire owne horses kept in the reare flanked with foote, marching by the edge of a Bogge,

& those horse they had gott from vs, sent away before with the fore-most of theire foote; when they sawe vs cominge, they turned heade & made readie to receiue vs, wee charged them, & at the first encounter I was stricken with a horseman's stafe in the Foreheade, in soe much as I fell for deade, & was a good while deprived of my sences: Butt the Captaines & Gentlemen that were about mee, where-of the cheife that I Remember were Captaine Anthony Elrington, Captaine John Sidney, Captaine John Kingsmyll, & Mathew Wroth, a Corporall of my horse Companie) gaue beyond my Bodie, & enforced them to giue ground a good way be meanes whereof I recouered myselfe, was sett vp on my horse & soe safelie brought of, & Conducted home, & they suffered with the prey they had gott to departe without further pursuite.

I kepte my Bedd of this wound by the space of a fortneth, my cham-ber a weeke after, & then I came abroade, & the first thinge I did, I tooke a viewe & particuler muster of all the Companyes. Howe weake I found them euen beyonnd expectation (though I had seene them decay very fast before,) is scarselie credible, & I thinke noe man will denye, but it was euen then a strange Companie, that of 150 in list could bring to doe seruice 25 or 30 able at the most.

Then did I alsoe manifestlie discouer the Trechery of the said Moyle Morrogh Mac Swynedo, (Mael-muire Mac Suibhne na d-Tuath,) hau-ing intercepted the Messanger that he imployed to O'Donnell in all his Bussines, out of whose mouth I gott a full Confession of all his Practices, & especiallie that it was hee, that caused his men of purpose to driue forth our horses, which he was so manifestlie convinced of as hee had not the face to denie it, wherevpon I deliuered him to Captaine Flemminge, who was then going to Dublin, to carry to my lord Deputie, there to recieue his tryall, who putting him vnder hatch-es in his shipp, & himselfe comiing to shoore with his Boate, the hatch being opened to sett Beere, he stept vp vpon the Decke, & threwe himselfe into the Riuer, and soe Swamme away to O'Cane's side, which was hard by; they in the shipp amazed with the sod-daynenesse of the fact, & doing nothing that tooke effect to prevent it.

On the 24th of August came Roory brother to O'Cane, (hauing before made his agreement with mee, to serue vnder Sr Arthur O'Neale) & brought with him 12 horse, 30 foote, & 60 fatt Beeues, a Present welcome at that time, for besides that fresh meate was then rare to be had, our provisions in stoore were very neere spent; I gaue him therefore a Recompence for them in money, & allowed him a small parte of souldiers to goe forth againe, whoe returned the next day & brought 40 more. Annother small Pray hee sett againe within fewe dayes after, & then thinking hee had gayned himselfe Credite enough, hee came & demaunded 800 men to doe an enterprise with-all, that should be (as he tould a very faire & probable tale for,) of farr greater importance & seruice to the Queene; I had onlie the persuation of Sr Arthur O'Neile (who I verylie thinke was a faithful & honnest Man,) granted him some men, though not halfe the Number he askt, because in truth I had them not. But before the time came they should sett forth, Sr Arthur had changed his opinion, & bad mee bewarre of him; I stayed my hand therefore, & refused him the men. He apprehended I did it out of distrust, & with many oathes & Protestations indeuored to perswade mee of his truth & fidelite; But finding all would not prevaile, he desired I would suffer him to goe alone with such men of his owne as he had, & he would retourne with such a testimonie of his honnestie, as I should neuer after haue Cause to be doubtefull of him more; I was content, soe hee left mee Pledges for his retourne, hee offered mee two that accepted of theire owne accords to engage their liues for it, & himselfe besids promised it with a solemne oath taken vpon the Bible, soe I lett him goe; The next day hee came backe to the waterside right ouer against the towne with 300 men in his Companye, and hauing the Riuer betweene him & vs, called to the souldiers on our side, & bad them tell mee, he was there returned according to promise; But ment noe Longer to serue against his owne Brother, & if for his Pledges I would accepte of a Ransome of Cowes, he would send mee in what reasonable Number I should demaund; But threatned If I tooke away their liues, there should not an English man escape, that euer came within his danger; This being presentlie brought vnto mee, & approved to be true by Repetition in myne own sight & hearing, I caused a Gibbett to be straight sett vp, brought them forth, & hanged them before his face, & it did after-wards manifestlie appeare, this man was of purpose sent in from the very beginning to betraye vs, & at this time he had laid soe faire a Plott, all was done by directions of Tyrone, who laye in Ambush to receiue vs.

And now the winter beganne to be feirce vpon vs, our men wasted with continuall laboures, the Iland scattered with Cabbins full of sicke men, our Biskitt all spent, our other prouisions of nothing but Meale, Butter, & a litle Wine, & that by Computation to hould out but 6 dayes longer. Tyrone and O'Donell, to weaken vs the more, Proclaming free passage & releife through theire Countrie to send them away to as many as would leaue vs and departe for England, our two fortes, notwithstanding all the dilligence wee had beene able to vse, farre from the state of being defensible, O'Donell well obseruing the opportunitie of this time, if his skill and Resolution had beene as good to prosecute it to the full, on the 16th of September came with 2000 Men about Midnight vndiscouered to the very edge of the Bogge, that divides the Iland from the mayne Lande, (for our horses were soe weake & soe fewe, that we were not able to hould watch any further out,) & there, being more then a good muskett shott of, they discharged theire peeces, whereby wee had warning enough (if neede had beene) to put our selues in Armes at leysure, But there was not a Night in many before wherein both myselfe & the Captaines satt not vp in expectation of this attempt, and Captaine Thomas White hauing some 20 horse readie in Armes for all occasions, came presentlie & brauelie Charged vpon the first that were now past ouer the Bogg & gott into the Iland, kild about 14 or 15, whose bodies wee saw lying there the next day, & the rest takeing a fright, confusedly retyred as fast as they could, yet to make it seene they departed not in feare they kepte thereabouts till the morning, & then assoone as it was broad day Light, they made a faire Parade of themselues vpon the side of a hill full in our sight & soe marched away.

The very next day came in a supplie of victuells, very shortlie after 50 newe horse, & shortlie after that againe 600 foote, & withall because the lords had been aduertized, the stoore-howses wee erected at first of Deale boardes onelie were many wayes insufficient & vnable to preserue the munitions & victuells in, they sent vs about this time two frames of Timber for howses, with most thinges necessarie to make them vp withall, which they ordayned to supplie that defect with & now alsoe where before the souldiers were enioyned to worke, without other allowance then theire ordinarie pays. Theire lordships vpon advertisment of the inconueniencie thereof (which in truth was such, as doe what wee could the workes went but exceedingly slowlie forward, & with very much difficulty), I then receiued order to give them an addition to theire wages (when they wrought vpon the fortifications) of 4*ds*, a day, & soe wee were then in all thinges fullie

& sufficientlie releeued.

On the third of October came in Neale Garvie O'Donell with 40 horse & 60 Foote, a man I was also directed by the state to winne to the Queene's seruice, & one of equall estimation in Tyrconnell that Sir Arthur O'Neale was of in Tyrone. The secreet messages that had past betweene him & mee, hee found were discouered to O'Donnell, & therefore somewhat sooner then otherwise he intended, & with less assuraunce & hope of many Conditions that hee stood vpon; yet it is true, I promised him in the behalfe of the Queene, the whole Countrey of Tirconnell to him & his heires, & my lord Deputie & Councell at Dublin did afterwards confirme it vnto him vnder theire hands, & his Coming in was very acceptable att that time, & such as wee made many vses of, & could ill haue spared.

The next day after hee came, wee drewe forth our forces, & made a iourney to the Isle of Inche, where, by his information, wee had learned there was a good Prey of Cattell to be gott; But the tides falling out extraordinaire high, wee were not able to pass them to gett in, so as wee were forced to turne our Course, & goe downe into O'Doghertie's Countrie, though to litle purpose; for knowing of our coming, hee draue away all before vs, onelie some stacks of Corne wee found, which wee sett on fire.

The 8th of October I assigned vnto the said Neale Garvie 500 foote & 30 horse, vnder the leading of Sr John Bowles, to goe to take the Liffer, where 30 of O'Donnell's men lay in Garrison in a Forte in one of the Corneres of the towne, & most of them being abroad when they came, were surpriced & slaine, & the place taken, yet soe as one of them had first putt fire into the Forte, which consumed all the Buildings in it, but the rest of the Howses scattered abroade in the towne (which were about 20) were preserued & stood vs afterwards in singuler good steade.

O'Donell having heard of the takeing of this Place, came on the xith of October with 700 foote & 100 horse, & encamped himselfe about 3 myles off at Castle Fyn. The next day he came & shewed himselfe before the Towne; our Garrison made out, had a skrimish with him of an houre longe, wherein Neale Garuie behaved himselfe Brauelie. Capten Augusten Heath tooke a light hurte in his hand, & some ten or twelve Men on ech side were slaine.

On the 24th he came againe & laide himselfe in ambush a myle from the towne, watching to intercept our men Fetching in of turfe, which before our Coming the Irish had made for theire owne provision. The Alarme taken, the Garrison made forth againe, & Neale Garvie behaued himselfe brauelie as before, charged home vpon them, killed one, hurt one or two more with his owne hande, & had his horse slaine vnder him. Captaine Heath tooke a shott in the thigh, whereof he shortelie after died, & some twenty more there were hurte & slaine.

On the 28th of October dyed Sr Arthur O'Neale of a fevour, in whose place came presentlie after one Cormocke, a brother of his, that clamed to succeed him as the next of his kinne, & had in that name good entertainments from the Queene; But shortelie after came his owne sonne, Tirlogh, that was indeed his true & imediate heire, whome the state accepted of & admitted to inherite all the fortune & hopes of his father. Hee had not attained to the full age of a man, & therefore the seruice he was able to doe was not greate, but some vse wee had of him, & I think his disposition was faithfull and honnest.

All this while after Liffer had been taken, O'Donell kept vp & downe in those parts, watching still to take our men vpon some advantage, but finding none, & hearing two Spanish shipps that were come into Calebegg (Killybegs) with Munition, Arms & Money, on the 10th of November he departed towards them, & betweene Tirone & him they made a Dividend of it.

After hee was gone, the Garrison both heere & at Dunalong sett diuers Preys of Catle, & did many other seruices all the winter longe, which I stand not vpon to make particuler mention of, & I must confess a truth, all by the help & advise of Neale Garvie & his Followers, & the other Irish that came in with Sr Arthur O'Neale, without whose intelligence & guidance litle or nothing could haue beene done of our selues, although it is true withall they had theire owne ends in it, which were always for priuate Revenge, & we ours to make vse of them for the furtherance of the Publique seruice.

And nowe came a practice of O'Donell's to open a discouverie, which had long beene mannaged in secret, & as he thought, Carried Close within the Compass of his owne & his associats' knowledge; Captaine Alford, that had the keeping of Culmore, fell into priuate familiaritie with Hugh Boy and Phelim Reogh (of the Septs of Mac Dauids), two Principall men about O'Doghertie, & of as good Credite & estimation with O'Donell. These men requested to haue leaue to buy Aquavitae, Cloath, and such other Comodities as that place afforded, which the Captaine and I, hauing our ends in it as well as they theires, gaue them free libertie to doe, & with more free access then any other, They measuring theire hopes by theire good entertainement, of all presentlie aboard him to knowe if hee would sell the Foarte, Hee seamed not vnwilling, soe he might be assured of some good & reall reward in hand; Many Meetinges & Consultations they had about it, & all with my knowledge. In the end it was resolued his Reward should be a Chaine of Gould in hand, which the Kinge of Spaine had formerlie giuen to O'Donell, & was worth aboute 8 scoore poundes, a 1000 Ir, in money the first day the Treason should be effected, & 3000 Ir, a yeare pention during his life, from the Kinge of Spaine; & for this he should onelie deliuer vpp the Foarte, with Neale Garvie in it, whome he should purposlie invite that Night to Supper. The time was sett & all thinges prepared; the Chaine, as a reall achiument of theire designe, I had delieured into my handes; But when the day came, they tooke a distast, & without aduenture of future loss, were contented to giue ouer theire bargaine. And about Christenmas this yeare dyed Sr John O'Doghertie in Tirconnell, being fledd from his owne Countrey with his goods & people, a man that in shewe seamed wonderfull desireous to yeald his obedience to the Queene, But soe as his actions did euer argue he was otherwise minded; But, it is true, O'Donell had at our first coming Ceazed his sonne, afterwards called Sr Cahir O'Doghertie into his hands, & kepte him as a Pledge vpon him which might iustly serue for some colour of excuse, that he was not at libertie to vse the freedom of his owne will; Being nowe deade, O'Donell sett vp in his place one Phelim Oge, a brother of his, neglecting the sonne who had bene bredd & fostred by the said Hugh Boye & Phelim Reaugh. These men tooke it as the highest iniurie [that] could be done vnto them, that theire Foster Child should be depriued of that, which they thought was his cleere & vndoubtible right, & therevpon seriouslie addressed themselves vnto Mee, and made offer, that in case I would maintaine the sonne against the Uncle, & Procure he might hold the Countrey, according to the same Lettres Pattents his father had it before him, they would worke the meanes to free him out of O'Donell's hands, to bring home the People & Catle that were fledd, & with them togeather with themselues, yeald obedience & seruice to the state; many messages & meetinges wee had about it, & none but to my knowledge; O'Donell was still made acquainted with, yea & with the very truth of euery particuler speach that past amongst vs; yet soe was he deluded (being himselfe a Crafte Master at that arte), that in the end a Conclusion was made betweene vs, theire demands were graunted by mee, & confirmed by my lord Deputie & Councell, hee perswaded to sett the young man at libertie; & when he had done, the people with theire goods retourned into the Countrie, took theire Leaues of him, & declared themselues for our side, & from that day forward wee had many faithfull & singuler good seruices from them, theire Churles & Garrans assistinge vs with Carriages, their catle, with plentie of fishe meate, & Hugh Boye & Phelim Reaugh with many intelligences & other helpes; without all which, I must freelie confess a truth, it had beene vtterlie impossible wee could haue made that sure & speedie Progress in the Warres that afterwardes wee did.

But therevpon begune Neale Garvie's discontentment, for presentlie he directed some men of his to be cessed vpon this Countrey; O'Doghertie & Hugh Boy with greate indignation refused to accept them. Complainte came before mee; I asked him wherevpon it was that hee challenged this power ouer annother man's land; he tould mee the land was his owne, for the Queene had giuen him all Tyrconnell, & this was part of it; I aunswered it was true, I know well the whole Countrey of Tyrconnell was promised him in as large & ample manner as the O'Donnells had beene accustomed to hould it: But I tooke it there were many others in that Countrey, that had lands of their owne as well as they, whose intrest I neuer conceiued was intended to be giuen to him; Hee replied not onelie the Countrey of Tyrconnell, but into Tyrone, Farmanaght, yea & Connaught, wheresoeuer any of the O'Donnells had at that time extended theire Power, hee mad Accompt all was his; hee acknowledged noe other kinde of right or intrest in any man else, yea the very persons of the People he challenged to be his, & said he had wronge, if any one foote of all that land, or any one of the Persons of the People were exempted from him. I saide againe these Demaunds were in my Judgement very vnreasonable, but hee should receive noe wronge by Mee; Let him haue Patience till wee might heare from my lord Deputie, & whatsoeuer his Judgement was I must & would obay; wounderfull impatient he was of any delay; but necessitie enforceing him, & the case sent to my lord, he returned this aunswere with the aduise of the Councell, that the vttermost could be challenged vpon the O'Doghertyes was but a chiefe Rent, sometimes paide to O'Neale, some times to O'Donnell; but that what-soeuer it were, they were of opinion was extinct euer since they held imediatelie from the Crowne, if Neale Garvie thought otherwise, his reasons should be heard with fauour when time should serue, & noe parte of that was promised him but should be made good; In the mean while he must be Contented, O'Doughertye must & should be exempted from him, which hee tooke with a greate deale more indignation & furie then became a man that was to raise his fortune onelie by the fauour of annother.

But the Springe coming now on, & having the helpe of this Countrey for Carriages, towards the latter end of March I drewe Forth & made a iourney vpon mac Swyne Fanaght, whose Countrie lyes diuided from O'Doghertye's by a Bay of the sea, I came vpon him vnawarrs, & surprised & gott into my possesion about 1000 of his Cowes before hee had Leasure to driue them away; Himselfe came vnto Mee vpon it, & desired his submission to the Queene might be accepted of, & vsed the mediation of O'Doghertye & Hugh Boy, that I would restore him the Prey, much entreatie & importunitie I was prest withall, & thinking with myselfe it might be a goode Example to such others as I should afterwards haue occasion to deale with, that I Sought not theire goods soe much as theire obedience (reserving a parte onelie for reward of the souldiers' labour,) I was contented & gaue him backe the rest, taking his oath, for his future fidelitie, & six pledges such as I was aduised to choose, & was borne in hand were very sufficient to binde him, & whereof his owne sonne was one; & to have a tye on him besids, I left Captaine Ralph Bingley, with his Company of 150 Men in Garrison in his Countrey, att the Abbay of Ramullan; It is true for all that, not long after without, Compulsion, he made his Reconciliation with O'Donnell vnder hand promised to betray the Garrison that lay vpon him, & secreetlie wrought to gett his Pledges out of my hand: But fayling in both, & yet, resolued to goe on his Course, he draue away all his Catle & goods, & openlie declared himselfe an Enymy against vs; In revenge whereof I presentlie hunge vpp his Pledges, & in September following made annother iourney vpon him, burnt & destroyed his houses and Corne, wherevpon Winter approaching insued the death of most of his People, & in December after, at the earnest entreatie of Neale Garuie, I tooke his Submission againe & sixe more Pledges, & from that for-ward he continewed in good subiection.

In the beginning of Aprill I made another iourney vpon them of

Sleught-art, a People that inhabited a Countrey in Tyrone of 16 myles longe, most parte Bogg & wood, & bordering not farr of from the Liffer, where onelie I had by Neale Garuie's meanes Castle-Derg deliuered into my hands, which I left Captaine Dutton in garrison in with his Companie of 100 men.

And then wee rested at home in expectation of a Supplie of Men from England against Sommer, for nowe were those wee had exceedinglie Wasted & decayed.

In the mean while O'Donell meditating a Revenge vpon Hugh Boy & O'Doughertie, & rightlie consideringe the advantage of the time, & the glorie & profitt he might gett to himselfe, & the dishonnor & loss he should bring vpon vs, if yet he could shew himselfe master of this Countrey, & be able to Prey it in dispite of our Protection, determined to make all the preparation hee could for that purpose, and had gathered togeather a faire & sufficient Armye (as he thought) to execute his designe withall; My care was as greate to Prevent him; I haue seene a Mapp of that Countrey, made by hand, by which it would appeare plaine to any man's viewe how this bussines was Carried; But for that which is ancient & Comon, it giues noe light at all, for it is vtterlie false, & hath not soe much as the Resemblance of the true situation of those partes, But pre-supposinge a sight of the better; in that place where the two Bayes of the sea that encompass it for the most parte, come to meete some what neere togeather, the distance of the land betweene them is about 6 myles broade, in a manner all Bogge, with a riuer passinge through from one side to the other, & not passable for horse nor any Numbers of foote, excepte in 5 or 6 Places, where there are certaine narrow foards of water to goe through, At one of the ends of this Necke of Land, stands an old broken Castle, called Coelmackatren, at the other an old fforte, called Cargan; into this, with a litle newe dressing, I put Captaine Thomas Badby, with his Companie; in the other Captaine Edmond Leigh, Vpon euery of the ffords I erected a small fforte, that held 20 men a Peece, such of the people as I suspected I sente for & kepte as Pledges, the goodes, which chiefelie consisted of Catle, & were, I thinke, about 3000 Cowes, I caused to be driuen to the further end next towardes Scotland, where a Peece of ground was inuironed with Sea able to Containe them at large for 3 or 4 dayes, the passage wherevnto by land was narrowe, & had an old ruined forte standing in it, which maimed as well without as within made it of a difficulte entrie: Heerevpon the first alarum, I gaue order the Catle should be driuen, & this place did Hugh Boy & his brother vndertake to defend with the aide of 200 English by the Powle, which were selected out of all the Companyes, & sent vnder the Comaund of Captaine Humphrey Willis; All thinges thus prepared on our side, O'Donell with his Army came & encamped, a mile from Cargan aforesaide, & seeing how I had fortefied the Passages, would not attempte to force any of them, but stayed att Least a weeke, makeing Heurdells out of a small Coppice thereabouts, & in the Night brought them vpon his Men's Backes, laide them in a place out of reach of our forts, & soe on the 7th May 1601 made his passage both for horse & foote ouer them, which noe sooner had beene done, but his men shooted for ioye, as thinking themselues most assured of theire prey; But when they found all driuen before them, & that he came downe to the Bottome of the Countrie, where he sawe our English ioyned with the Natiues, readie to defend the Place, with the Catle behinde them, hee made a stoppe & encamped close before them, the next day gaue an assalt, & was repulsed, attempted againe, & sawe 40 of his men slaine, then out of hope to doe good, trussed vp Baggage, & not one Cowe ritcher then hee came in, made his retreate backe againe, Going out hee past by Coelmackatren vpon the stronde, at a dead lowe water, where our Men had a litle skrimish with him, vnder succcor of the Castle, & where I came with some few horse & foote to see what Countenance hee held in his departure; Being cleane past I sawe his men drawe into Battaile, & I thinke that noe man that sawe them aswell as I, but will confess they were not fewer then 1500; Phelim Reagh in this assalt that was giuen behaued himselfe brauely with his owne handes, Hugh Boy honnestlie acquitted himselfe in all this occasion, & both of them gaue sufficient testimonye theire hearts were at that time faithfull, and Zealous to the Queene's seruice.

The very same day they past away by Coelmackatren, the shipps were discouered to the mouth of Loughfoile that brought vs a new supplie of 800 men.

Then on the 24th of May I drewe two Iron peeces to Newtowne, a Castle in Tyrone, 6 myles distant from the Liffer in the way to Dongannon; this I beate vpon all one day, & the next morning had it deliuered vp; It is a Pile of stone strong & well built, with an Iron Gate & Chaine att the doore, it hath before it a large Bawne compast with a good high Stone wall, & in the middest of it a fairie Irish thacht

house, able to hould 50 or 60 men in it. Heere I left Captaine Roger
Atkinson in Garrison with his Companie of 100 men, & because one
of the cheifest vses wee intended these Garrisons for was to make suddaine Inroades vpon the Countrey, to Spoyle & pray them of theire
Catle, & that impossible to be done without intelligence & Guidance
of some of the Natiues, I left to assist him in that kinde one Tirlogh
Magnylson, a man that came in with Sr Arthur O'Neale, that had
often guided our men before in like seruices, & had gayned himselfe
a great deale of loue & reputation amongst vs, & had now the
Comaund of 100 Irish by my lord Deputies allowance; I gaue speciall
charge, he should be lodged cleane without the Bawne, & notwithstanding all his Credite a warry & circumspect Eye should be Carried
vpon him.

About the 20th of June, I brought the Demy Cannon I had, to
Ainogh, a Castle of O'Caines, standing in a lough, not much aboue a
myle from the Derrey, but the riuer betweene, with which I beate
vpon it, the first day a good distaunce of, & did litle good, but at night
wee drewe the Battery within 80 pase, & the next morninge wee
founde the ward was runne out of it. Heere I receiued lettres from my
lord Deputy, propounding to my choise, by way of discourse, two
mayne seruices to spend this sommer vpon, the one the takeing of
Ballyshannon, the other the meeting him at Blackwater, for
Ballyshannon I had many reasons to refuse it, for the other imagyning
noe impediment but the want of powder, perhappes, because I knewe
in the takeing of these Castles a greate deale had beene spente, I called
the Clarke of the munition to Mee, & asked him howe he was stoored
of Powder, he tould mee hee had 60 Barrells; I was fullie satisfied in
my minde, I enquired noe further, But returned my aunswere, In any
parte of Tyrone, I should be readie to meete him, wheresoeuer hee
pleased.

The 19th of July at the Derrey, I receiued two lettres togeather, one
dated the 9th, the other the 14th of the same Moneth, by the first I
was willed to prepaire myselfe to this iourney, by the second to make
hast a waye, because his lordship was there & expected Mee; I presen-
lie gaue order the Companies should drawe to Liffer, & come fur-
nished with Munition; word was brought mee they could gett noe
Match; I called for the Clarke, & asked him the Reason, hee tould
mee hee had it not; noe, said I, did yow not tell Mee the other day,
yow had 60 Barrells? I tould yow, saide hee, that I had 60 Barrells of

Powder & soe I had, but of Match yow asked mee nothing; I demaunded if a Barrell of Match were not alwayes sent as a due Proportion to
a Barrell of Powder, hee Confest it was, & ought to be soe, but much
of that came hee saide, was rotten & much had beene wasted, soe as
nowe hee had it not; I asked him why hee tould mee not soe much,
when I spake of it the other day, hee said because my question, was of
powder onelie & nothing of Match. Captaine Humphrey Covert was
then going for England, I examined him in his presence, & desired he
would be a witness, to what hee sawe & heard, badd him send to all
the Garrisons for that hee had, & bring it togeather to the Liffer when
he had soe done, there was but 6 Barrells of it in all, & they short to,
of that they ought to Containe, I then propounded to the ancientest
of the Captaines, what they would advise mee to doe, to faile my lord
I sawe myselfe iustlie ly open to a greate deale of Reprochfull Censure,
to ingage the Army with soe greate a want, how might I aunswere it;
They gaue theire oppinions, subscribed with theire handes, the proportion was a greate deale to litle to gett forth withall, for they knewe
O Donnell & all the Countrey thereabouts were alreadie assembled to
attend vs, & by all likeliehood would prouoke vs to skrimish by the
way, & it was better to incurre any Censure of the world whatsoeuer,
then to expose soe many Men to be a Butt onelie for theire Enymyes
to shoot att; Therevpon I sent Lieuetenant Goordon to my lord with
lettres, declaring the accident, desireing suspension of Judgement till
truth might be fullie examined, & offerring vpon perill of my life to
come yett to the place, soe afterwardes, his lordship would furnish
mee to returne againe. His aunswere was this, your wants are small in
shewe, in substance greate, how this will be taken in England, that
yow made them not knowne before the instant when it was impossible to supplie them, it behoues yow to looke vnto, for mee, I must
confess yow haue much deceiued my expectation, but I will not aduise
yow to doe anythinge, with the Queene's Army that is not warrantable
by good reason, neither trust vpon Mee to helpe yow heere, for I ame
not able, but if you can, take some other oppurtunitie of seruice to
make amends withall.

Now had O'Donnell, O'Caine, Cormocke mac Baron, & all the
Cheifes of the Countrie thereabout made all the forces they were able,
to attend the issne of this intended Meeting of my lord and Mee, and
had drawne themselues togeather about Cormocke mac Barron's
country, where they might be readie to fall vpon either of vs, as they

should see theire best advantage; & conferring with Neale Garuie, I then found by O'Donnell's absence, the countrie behinde him was left without gaurd, the Abbay of Dunnagall was kepte onelie by a fewe fryers, the situation of it close to the Sea, & very Convenient for many seruices, especiallie for a stepp to take Ballyshannon with, which was a worke, the manifould attempts & chargeable Preparations the Queene had been att to accomplish, & my lord himselfe had soe latelie aymed att, & valued equall to this other of meeting him at Blackwater, did argue would be of speciall importance & good acceptation; I concluded therefore, & sent him away (the said Neale Garvie) with 500 English souldiers to put themselves into this place, which they did on the 2nd of August.

On the 6th August I receiued a supplie of 200 Bundells of Match from Sir Arthur Chichester from Knockfergus, & my lord hauing shortlie after performed at Blackwater what his intentions were, according to the opportunitie of that time, withdrewe his Army; And then O'Donnell with those forces he had, returned & laide seige to these men which Continewed at least a moneth, & in the meane time on the 19th of September, the Abbay tooke fire, by accident or of purpose, I could neuer learne, but burnt it was, all saue one Corner, into which our men made Retreate, & through, the middest of the fire were forced to remoue their Provisions of victuell & the very barrells of Powder they had in stoore Captaine Lewis Oriell comanded in cheife; The face of this night's worke (for the fire beganne in the Eueninge) is easilie to imagination to behould, O'Donnell's men assayling, & ours defendinge, the one wth as much hope, the other with as good a resolution, as the accident on the one side, & the necessitie on the other gaue occasion for; The next day when the fflame was spent, & that it appeared our men had gott a Corner of the house, which nowe stood by itselfe, & out of Danger to be further annoyed by the fire, O'Donnell sent Messengers of sumons vnto them, offered them faire Conditions to departe, terrified them with his strength, & theire impossibilitie to be releeved; but all in vaine, theire passage to the sea was still theire owne, by land they sent mee word of theire estate & violentlie repelled his Messenger; Heere againe I must confess Neale Garvy behaued himselfe deservinglie, for though I had at that time many informations against him, that could not but breed some iealousies of his fidelitie; yet wee sawe he Continewed to the last, tooke such parte as our men did, had many of his men slaine at this seige, & amongst the rest a brother of his owne.

Togeather with the Newes of this accident, came annother that Newtowne was betrayed by Tirlogh Magnylson; This man hauing the Night before guyded our Men to the fetching of a Prey, came the next day & dyned with the Captane, inticed him to walke forth vpon the greene before the howse, lead him purposlie as farre as he could, & on the suddaine, with the helpe of 3 or 4 of his men, that followed him, Ceized him theire Prisoner, att the same instant two others had gott in vpon the Centynell at the Castle-doore, & the rest att the Bawne-gate suddenlie brake in, fell vpon the Souldiers, lying in the Irish thatched house & put them euery man to the Sword.

And in like manner and vpon the same day was Captaine Dutton alsoe Betrayed at Castle Derreg, saue that the souldiers lives weere onelie saued.

Ffor these losses there was noe reamidy for the present, for Dunnagall I had before sent them provisions by sea which came to them in due time, & in a reasonable manner supplied most of theire wants, for the rest I could doe nothing but encourage them to hould it, & assured them to come to theire aide soe soone as they should stande in neede it.

But now came the newes of the Spanyards arrivall at Kinsaile, whereupon O'Donnell brake upp the seige, to march towards them, Tyrone made hast the same way, and soe alsoe did my lord Deputie, and it is true, the Countrey was nowe left voide and noe powerfull Enymy to encounter withall more then the Rivers, and the difficulties of the passage of the wayes.

And then, finding a fitt opportunitie for it, I fraim'd a iourney vpon O'Caine, soe as I entred vpon him two wayes at once Captaine Roger Orme with 2000 Men past ouer at Greene-Castle in O'Doghertye's Countrie by boate, & with the rest of the forces drewe vp to the Cannon, a wood that streacheth all a long the front of his Countrey as yow pass into it from the Derrey thowrough which was a pase guarded at that time by Rorie O'Caine with 300 Men, (of whose trecherie mention is made before). This man comes with 40 horse, & brand it a quarter of a myle before his strength Edmond Groome, a brother to Hugh Boy & Phelim Reagh, steppes out to encounter him. Roory slipps of from his horse, & beganne to runne away on foote, the other alights and pursues him, catches him by the Collor, & in veiwe of vs all bringes him backe, & delivers him to mee. I badd the

Souldiers presentlie kill him, & soe without any greate resistaunce wee entred into the Countrey, which wee found large & full of howses & Corne; we diuided our selfes, one halfe toward the Band, one other half went forthright, & Captaine Orme tooke all alonge the sea shoore & sett a Compass about soe as at night wee mett altogeather and encamped in the middest of the Countrey, ech severall troupe hauing fired the houses & Corne they mett withall, which I neuer sawe in any place in more aboundance. The next day wee diuided our selues againe, wasted what wee found more, tooke some Cowes, but very many sheepe & other small Catle, & with much Pillage, which the Souldiers loaded themselues withall. Discerning nowe that the weather inclyning to a thawe, (for at first it was a hard frost,) [wee] made homeward, & with much adoe could attaine to repass those Riuers, which wee found dry in a manner when wee first came in.

And now being earnestlie called vpon for a supplie of victuells by them at Dunnagall, (the second shipping I had sent about for that purpose, being kept backe with foule weather,) I tooke vp Garrons in O'Doghertie's Countrey, loaded them with salte & Biskett, & with 100 Beeues went ouer the mountaines, most parte on foote, the wayes were soe rotten, & on the 12th Day of December brought them releife; & because I sawe that litle pyle reserued from the rage of the fire too small a greate deale to containe a large & important Garrison, I remoued parte of them, & added two Companys moore to ly at Ashrowe, an Abbay 10 myles further, & not aboue a quarter of a Myle distant from Ballyshannon; left Captaine Edward Digges, the Sergiant Maior to Commaund there, tooke a viewe of the Castle, promised as soone as I came home to send him the Demy cannon, which before I had taken Ainogh withall, gaue my oppinion howe he should proceede in the vse of it, tooke oath & pledges of the cheife of the Inhabitants thereabouts, & soe returned. By the way I was a litle stopped by the passage of the waters, & before I came home, the Newes ouertooke Mee of the Lord Deputie's happie victorie att Kinsaile, of Tyrones flight and returning homewards, & of O'Donell's departure to Sea to goe into Spaine. I sent away the Cannon assoone as I came home, & on the 20th of March it arrived there, & on the 25th (being the first day of the yeare 1602) was that long desired placed taken by the said Captaine Digges, with less then a tenth parte of that charge which would haue beene willinglie bestowed vpon it, & the Consequence thereof brought many furtherances to the gennerall seruice.

And now had I a good while before entertayned a partie, that vndertooke to deliuer mee Tirlogh Magnylson (that betrayed the Castle of
Newtowne) togeather with as many of his men as were Guiltie of that
bloodie treason, either deade or aliue. They protracted time as I
thought, yet it was not full 4 moneths, after they had vndertooke it,
before they had kild many of his People as they trauelled single vp &
downe in the Countrey, & noe man knewe who did it, some of them
alsoe came into my hands aliue, whome I caused the Souldiers to hewe
in peeces with theire swordes; & nowe at last hee himselfe alsoe was
lighted vpon; His custome was alwayes (for feare of betraying) to goe
forthe alone in the Eueninge, & in some old house or other in the
wood, kindle a fire, & make as though he ment to lye there, after a
while remoue & doe as much in annother, & soe from house to house
3 or 4 times, or more perhapps as his minde gaue him.

A Boy was sent to watch him, who often brought these Men word
where hee was, but still when they came they missed, & found hee was
gone to some other place, yet in the end hee dogged him soe close,
that after divers remoues, hee lookt in & sawe him pull of his trows-
es, & ly downe to sleepe, then came, & tould them of it, & fower of
them togeather armed with Swordes, Targetts, and Murrions, fell in
vpon him, hee gat up his Sword for all that, & gaue such a Gash in
one of theire Targetts as would seame incredible to be done with the
arme of a Man, but they dispacht him & brought mee his heade the
next day, which was presentlie knowne to euery Boy in the Armey, &
made a ludibrious Spectacle to such as listed to behould it. I gaue
them a good some of money in hand for theire Reward, & promised,
the warrs ended, they should enioy such landes as they & theire Septe
had beene accustomed to dwell vpon, & assurance of favour & protection from the state.

Tirlogh, alsoe, the sonne of Sir Arthur O'Neale, procured mee the
Castle againe, onelie desiring whensoeuer the Garrison, I would put
in it, should be withedrawne, it might not be deliuered into any Man's
handes but his, as being a parcell of his owne peculier & Patrimonall
landes, which I faithfullie promised him it should not.

Ffor them of Sleught Art alsoe that betrayed Captaine Dutton, I
brought them to come in & profess theire obedience by oath, & deliuery of Pledges, which notwithstandinge they afterwardes brake, & I
sett them in againe, with the most profound execrations vpon themselues, if they continewed not true, that the tongue of Man was able

to express, & yet for all that they flewe out againe, & all the reamidie I could haue, was to wast & spoile theire Countrey, & destroy theire people, which I did with all the extremitie I could, & yet the two cheife of them which were the Ringleaders of the rest, doe what I could escaped with theire liues & kepte vp an downe in the woodes euen till Tyrone was taken to Mercie, & they particulerlie pardoned with him, by my lord Deputyes express Comaund.

On the 20th of Aprill, I made an agreement with Caue Ballogh (Cumhaighe Ballach) mac Rickard a Cheife Gentleman in O'Caine's countrie who deliuered mee the Castle of Dongevin, situate neere vpon the Glinnes, & about 18 myles wide from the Derrey; the warres ended I gaue my word that it should be restored againe.

In May, I receiued diuers lettres from my lord Deputie, all in discourse about his intent of coming that sommer to Blacke water againe, where hee willed I should prepare myselfe to meete him; And the lords from England had now sent vs annother supplie of 800 men, that landed att Derrey about the latter ende of this Moneth.

And soe on the 16th day of June, from Liffer I sett forth to meete him; But when wee had Marched two dayes, & lay in Campe att Terwin Mac Guirk, I vnderstoode hee would not be readie till 6 dayes after, thereupon I returned backe, & hauing discouered by myne Eye as I past by it the day before, that Omy was a place easie to be fortefied, & stood convenient for many vses, to leaue a Garrison in, I made it Defensible with fower dayes' labour, & left Captaine Edmond Leigh solye in it, on the 26th I sett forward againe, & encamped 4 Myles shorte from Dongannon, & going forth with some horse to discouer, I mett with my lord's skowts that Conducted mee that night to his Campe.

The next day Sir Arthur Chichester came ouer at Lough Sidney [Lough Neagh], & landed 1000 Men at that place, where he presentlie erected a fforte, which had afterwards the name giuen it of Mountioy, & my lord hauing gayned his passage before and erected annother at Blackwater, which he called by the name of Charle Mounte, the axe was nowe at the roote of the tree, & I may well say, the Necke of the Rebellion as good as vtterlie broken, for all that Tyrone was afterwardes able to doe, was but to saue himselfe in places of difficult access vnto.

Ten dayes (as I remember,) I stayed with his lordship in these partes, assisting him to spoyle & wast the Countrey, which he indeuored by all the meanes hee could possible to doe, & then my prouision of victuell spent hee gaue mee leaue to retourne, with order to be in a readines againe to meete him about a Moneth after.

I was noe sooner come home to the Derrey, But O'Caine sent Mee an offer of his submission, I acquainted my lord withall, hee bad mee dispatch & make shorte with him, that wee might be the readier for a Mayne Prosecution vpon Tyrone: soe on the 27th of July, wee came to a full agreement, the substance whereof was this (Countersigned with ech of our handes,) that soe much of his Countrey as ley betweene the Riuers of Foghan, Bangibbon, & Loughfoyle, should be to her Maiestie to dispose of to whome shee pleased; a peece of Ground should be allotted for maintenance of a Garrison at the Band, the rest he should haue her Maiestie's lettres Pattents for, to hould to him & his heires. These Conditions my lord acknowledged to be better then hee looked for, approued them vnder his hand, promised mee the inheritaunce of the reserued lands, & gaue mee the present vse & Custodium of it vnder the Exchequer Seale, & him the like of the rest, then wrote vp to mee, to drawe vp to the Omy, to wast all the Countrie I could thereabouts, & there to attend him against hee sent vnto Mee againe.

On the 10th of August I came thither, & Hugh Boy, coming after mee the next day, was sett vpon & slaine by a partie of loose fellowes that fell vpon him by chaunce; A man whome I found faithfull & honnest, let Enuie & Ignuoraunce say what they will to the Contrarye. Hee left three brothers behinde him, Phelime Reaugh, Edmonde Groome, & Shaine Cron; they were all men of very good parts, & deserued a better Countenance at least from the state then my Creditt was able to procure them, which if they had had, & those Courses forborne that Phelime Reaugh was vext withall, by particuler Persons, vpon no sufficient ground of reason, that I ame wittnes to, theire liues had perhappes beene preserued to this day, & a better oppinion conceiued of vs in gennerall then is, by the rest of that Nation. Let noe man Censure mee a misse for this kinde of saying; for I hould it a sinne to Conceale a truth where I ame interested & haue occasion to speake it.

Being heere, & knowing my lord was not yet readie to take the feild, I was tould by Irish Guides of a prey that in theire opinion was easilie to be sett out of Cormocke mac Baron's Countrey, & I liked theire reasons soe well, that I resolued to giue an attempte for it. Soe I tooke

out 400 foote & 50 horse, & sett forth in the eueninge & Marcht all
Night; by breake of the day wee found it was gone further then they
made accompte of, & loath to retourne Emptie, wee followed it till
wee were at least 3 myle from home, Captaine Edmond Leigh that
Comaunded the vaunt Guard, with a fewe light horse & foote in the
ende ouertooke it gaurded by Cormocke himselfe, whome he
presentlie charged & beate away; then went in & gathered about 400
Cowes togeather, & brought them to vs where wee made a stande with
the Mayne forces. Wee were then all exceeding wearie, & therefore
finding howses at hand, satt downe & rested our selues a while. After
wee risse, & had marched about three Myle, wee might discerne
troupes of Men gathered togeather in Armes drawing towards a wood
which wee must pass thorowgh, to possess themselues of it before vs.
I then allighted, sent away my horse, & put myselfe in the Rere, badd
the rest of the horse with a fewe foote & the Prey make hast & gett
thorowgh as fast as they Could, & soe they did before there came
downe any greate Numbers vpon them; Upon vs that came after with
the foote, they fell with a Crye, & all the terrour they were able to
make, skirmisht with shott, till all our Powder on both sides were
spente; then came to the sword & Push of Pike, & still as wee beate
them off, they would retyre, & by & by come vpon vs againe. These
kindes of assaults I thinke I may safelie say, they gaue us at least a
dozen of; yet in the end wee carryed our selues cleere out, came to a
place where our horse made a stand vpon a faire large, & hard peece
of ground. There wee put ourselues into order or Battaile, drewe forth
againe & Marched away; they stoode in the edge of the woode, &
gaue vs the lookeing on, but offered to follow vs noe further; soe we
lodged quietlie that Night, & the next day came home to Omy where
wee diuided our Prey, withein 20 of the full Number of 400 Cowes,
& found wanting of our Men about 25. The pase we went through
was a good Myle longe, the wood high Oaken Timber, with some
Coppice amongst it, & most of the wayes nothing but dirte & myre.
O'Doghertie was with vs, alighted when I did, kept mee companie in
the greatest heate of the feight, beheaued himselfe brauelie, & with a
great deale of loue & affection, all that day, which at my next meeting
with my lord, I recommended him for, & he gaue him the honnor of
knighthoode in recompence of; And so of the Captaines & officers,
there was not one but was well putt to it, & had none other meanes
to quitt himselfe by, but his owne Valour; And these I can nowe call

to Remembrance were Captaine Leigh, Captaine Badby, Captaine Ralph Bingley, Captaine John Sidneye, Capt William Sidney, Captaine Harte, & Ensigne Davyes, that was shott in the theigh, & not without Difficulty brought of & afterwards safelie cured.

Shortley after my lord wrote vnto Mee, he was almost readie for the feilde againe, & had a purpose to plante a Garrison at Clogher or Aghar, both standing on this Cormocke's landes, willed mee, if I could, to bringe a peece of Artillery with mee, & as much victuell as I was able, & soe be in a readines against the next time I should heare from him. Artillery I was not able to bring, but about 10 dayes after I came to him, about 8 myles wide from Dungannon, &, as I remember, founde Sir Arthur Chichester with him, but sure I ame, wee mett all three about that time, & marched togeather about 6 or 7 dayes in which time the Castle of Aghar standing in a lough 12 myles wide from Omy was yealded to him, & he placed Captaine Richard Hansard in Garrison in it, with 20 dayes victuell, & lefte mee in charge to supplie him when that time came out, which I did to the very day Tyrone was taken in, & order giuen for restitution of it into his handes; & afterwardes when wee parted, hee sent Sir Hen Follyatt with Mee to Comaund att Ballyshannon, first with directions to be vnder Mee, but not long after to be absolute Gouernor of himselfe.

As I came home, finding avoydance by a ward in a Castle of Harry Hovodin's, 3 myles from the Newtowne, & standing in a loughe, seeing a peece of grounde that Comaunded iust vpon the gate, I drewe a trench, & lodged Musketeers, that did nothing but beate vpon it, & left Captaine Nicholas Pynner with two Companys to plye them, whoe did it soe well, that within 14 dayes the place was giuen vp, & because I would not trouble myselfe with the care of Victuelling it, I pulled it downe & raised it to the ground.

And shortelie after this, was Roory O'Donnell, brother to O'Donnell that was fledd into Spaine (and himselfe banished his Countrey & living in Connaught,) taken in by my lord Deputie, a profest enymy to Neale Garvy, who apprehended such Jealousies vpon it, as made him runne Courses that were afterwards his vndoing. It gaue an occasion to make it be thought, Tyrone alsoe should be taken to Mercye, & thervpon O'Caine came vnto Mee, & requested I would write vnto my lord, that in case hee were, his lordship would please to Remember, he had promised him to be exempted from him, & that hee desired hee would bee as good as his word; I thought it needless, but yet at his importunitie I did soe, & receiued this answere, that his lordship knewe not yett whither hee should be taken in or noe, but if hee were, beleeve mee, said hee, O'Caine shall be free & exempted from him. Wee both then rested securelie satisfied from all further doubts.

On the 18th of November I receiued an advertisment from Sir Arthur Chichester, that Tyrone had betaken himselfe to the Glynnes, & that his opinion was, if hee were well sett vpon by both of vs togeather, his heade might perhappes be gott, or at least he might be driuen & forced out of that place; wee discoursed vpon it by lettres, & agreed to giue the attempte, & on the 18th of December, with all the forces I was able to make, which was 50 horse, 450 English foote, 200 of O'Caines, & 100 of O'Doghertyes Kearne, Neale Garvie beinge then & longe before estraunged from Mee, I came to Dongannon, which is 5 Myles shorte from the entrie of the Glinnes.

The first day I lay still, & gaue aduertisment onelie to Sir Arthur Chichester of my coming, whoe was (as I imagined) newe come to the other side. The next day I went vp to a Mountaine 4 Myle off, where I viewed them with myne Eye, & it seamed (as wee were tould before) they were ten Myle broade, & 20 Myle longe, all Couered with thicke wood, and questioning with my guides about the course I should hould to make my Entry into them, I found nothing but varietie & contradiction of opinions, & therefore the next day after, at night, I appointed Captaine Ralph Bingley with 100 light English, & most of O'Caine's & O'Dohertye's Kearne, to goe in as farre as they could, & bring Mee certaine word how the wayes were. They had not gone aboue a Myle, but the Irish mutyned, & for noe perswation would goe any further, & O'Caine's men plainelie brake off & went home to theire howses: O'Dougherties returned to the Campe, but firmelie maintayned the wayes were not passable. Upon the 23rd I held a Consultation with the Captaines, & conferred with our Guides in theire presence, & thus by concurrance of voyces wee gathered from them of the most certaintie, but there was noe way possible to come neere to Tyrone, but wee must first for one daye's iourney abandon all Carriadge but what wee had on our backes, & incampe one night in the woodes; that att our first entrance wee must pass a brooke, which if rayne fell, wee could not repass againe till it ceased; That Tyrone lay plasht all about with trees, & had sente most of his Cowes to Sleugh-Gillen, where it would be in vaine to make after them. And demaunding theire oppinions herevpon, they all agreed, seeing the Irish soe backward, and these inconveniences withall, It were better to leaue good store of Irish to ply him with contynuall Stealthes, & they thought it would weaken him more, & be a safer Course, then to attempte him with these mayne forces, & that att the vttermost, it could not bee above 2 or 3 Monethes, before of himselfe, hee would be forced out of that place to a more open Countrey, where he might be dealt withall better Cheape. Yet if Sir Arthur Chichester thought otherwise, & would on his parte resolue on a day to enter on his side, lett them haue knowledge of it, & all excuses sett aparte, vpon perill of theire liues, they would meete him or lye by the way. I presentlie sente away my lettres with aduertisment of this resolution of theires, & attending an aunswere, on the 26th I receiued one from him dated the night before, wherein he wrote he had heard but one from Mee, & that was at my first Coming, woundred at it, & desired to knowe my resolution, setting downe 4 dayes longer to stay for it, & then if it came not to be gone; whereby it appeared that most of my lettres were miscarried, for it was well knowne there had not one Night past after I came, but I writt & made one dispatch or other vnto him, & the next day our principall Guide (to encrease the suspition) came away from vs & went to Tyrone. Annother knowing that 30 Cowes were coming to Mee vpon the way, from the Derrey, went & intercepted them, & followed the same way. A Rumor was raised alsoe that Neale Garvie had prey'd the Liffer, & lastlie our strenght was nowe decreased at least 50 Men that were fallen sicke. The Consideration of these thinges added to the former, made vs then to send word againe, he should not stay vpon vs, for wee were fullie resolued to turne home, & soe wee did, leaving behinde vs 100 Irish that vndertooke to be still doing vpon him, & presentlie after placeing a Garrison att the Band, both to stopp his traffique that was for many necessaries, that hee could not well liue without, as alsoe to prevent his escape by Sea, if he should attempt it, as I was crediblie aduertised he was in consultation to doe: Besides I had intertained diuers that seuerallie vndertooke to deliuer Mee his heade. I knewe Sir Arthur Chichester had done the like, & soe attending the opportunitie that time should offer being come home to the Derrey, this bussines came in my way to deal in.

Neale Garvie (as I said before) had a longe time carryed himselfe discontented, estrainged himselfe from mee, & liued altogeather in those partes about Ballyshannon, & it is true, those seruices he had done, alwayes dulie acknowledged, I had very often & very bitterlie Complayned of him to my lord, & my Reasons were these: Hee did openly & contynuallie contest with Mee to haue the people sworne to him and not to the Queene; To haue noe officer whatsoeuer but him-selfe in his Countrey; Hee would not suffer his men to sell vs theire owne goodes, nor worke with vs for Money, nor till or sowe the ground any where neere vs, nor yeald vs any Carriages for the Army, as O'Doghertye, and all other that were vnder the Queene did: yea he hath taken Cowes from his People vnder noe other Colour but because hey haue come to Mee when I haue sent to speake with them; Diuers stealthes haue beene made vpon vs, whereof it hath beene proued he had his shaire, & nothing more Comon with him, then to receiue & Conceale Messengers from Tyrone, & O'Donell, & when he hath first denyed it, & afterwards had it proued to his face, his onelie excuse was he refused theire offers. Hee would not endure that any Man of his Countrey should be punished for any Cryme, though neuer soe haynous, & manifestlie proued; but take it as the highest iniurie could be done vnto him. His Entertainements were about 12£ a day, for himselfe & the Men hee had in pay, & yett would muster but when hee list, and sometimes absolutelie not at all; Many Misdemeanors there were in him of this kinde, & many friendlie per-swations haue I vsed to reforme them, that done, his greatnes in the qualitie of a subiect, I neither did nor had reason to Envie. Now it fell out that my lord wrote for Rorie O'Donnell to come to him to Dublin; Hee being in Connaught, desires first to putt ouer his Catle into Tirconnel, which would otherwise be in danger in his absence to be preyd by those of that prouince that yett stood out in Rebellion; my lord giues him leaue, & writes to Neale Garvie that hee shall not molest nor trouble them, & soe Roory takes his Journey. Hee was noe sooner gone, & the Catell put ouer. But Neale Garvie, notwithstand-ing my lord's Comaund, Ceizes them as his owne, vnder pretents they were the goods of the Countrey belonging vnto him. Complainte made, my lord writes to Me to see them restored: I send vnto him & hee refuseth. My lord vpon that bidds Mee discharge him of his Entertainements, & writes vnto him without delay to come to him to Dublin. Hee growes more discontented, & deferres his going. Thus it runnes on for at least 3 Monethes togeather, & neither would he come to Mee nor my lord, nor by any meanes be perswaded to make Restitution. In the ende he assembles of his owne aucthoritie all the

Countrey att Kilmackoran [Kilmacrenan], a place where the
O'Donnells vse to be chosen; There hee takes vpon him the title, &
with the Ceremonyes accustomed, proclaymes himselfe O'Donell, &
then presentlie comes to Mee to the Derrey, with a greater troupe of
attendances then at any time before, & they styling him at euery word
my Lord. Assoone as I sawe him, I asked him howe he was thus suddenlie stept into the Name of a lord: hee tould Mee they called him
so because he was O'Donnell. I asked him by what aucthoritie he was
soe, & hee said by my lord Deputies; I badd him make that appeare
vnto Mee & all was well. Hee pluckt out a lettre written vnto him
from my lord about two yeares before, Superscription whereof was
this, 'To my very loving friende O'Donnell;' I asked him if this were
all the Warrante hee had, & hee said yes. I asked him why he went not
to my lord all this while, nor came vnto Mee sooner, nor restored
Rorie O'Donell's Catle. His aunswere was this; you knowe the whole
Countrey of Tirconnell was long since promised Mee, & many
seruices I haue done, that I thinke haue deserued it, but I sawe I was
neglected, & therefore I haue righted myselfe, by takeing the Catle, &
People, that were my owne, & to preuent others, haue made myselfe
O'Donnell; now by this meanes the Countrey is sure vnto Mee; & if
I haue done any thinge amisse, lett all be pardoned that is past, &
from this day forward, by Jesus' hand, I will be true to the Queene, &
noe Man's Councell will I follow hereafter but yours. You take a
wronge Course, said I, it may not goe thus, the first act yow must doe
to procure forgiunes for your faults (if it may be) is to make restitution of the Catle; if you doe it not of your owne accord, I knowe yow
will be forced vnto it vpon harder Conditions. Yet at that time nothing I could say would prevaile with him, & soe hee departed downe
into the towne; And of all these manner of Proceedings I writt vnto
my lord: But it is true the next day hee came & made offer to restore
them, & I was glad of it, & sent for Rory O'Donnell (who was then
at the Liffer) to come and receiue them, & my thoughts were fullie
bent to make the best Reconsilation of the Bussines that I could.
Roory came but with open Clamour, that Neale Garvie had laide a
Plott to murther him by the way, & it is true, if the Confession of 3
of his owne Men may be beleeued, he was the Night before in
Consultation to haue it done, but did not (as they say) Resolue vpon
it: but this put all the Bussines out of fraime, for then could wee get
Roory to noe kinde of Patient Conferrence, & in the meane time

came lettres from my lord to this effect, that hee had now taken in Tyrone, & was fullie resolued to beare noe longer with Neale Garuie, and therefore if I were sure he had made himselfe O'Donnell, it was treason by the lawe, I should lay hould on him & keepe him safe. My lord, I was sure, was mistaken in the qualitie of his offence, for I looked vpon the Statute Booke, & sawe that Rigerous lawe was onelie for such as made themselues O'Neales, for those that looke vpon them to be heads of other families, the Punishment was onelie a Penaltie of 100 marks. I pawsed therefore & was doubtefull with myselfe, whither by this Misgrounded warraunt I should doe well to restrayne him or noe. But while I stood aduising vpon it, Came others lettres of aduertisement of the Queene's death, & order to Proclame the kinge. Then I entred into a further Consideration, should this man take the aduantage of the time, & knowinge he hath offended the state, stepp aside & take Armes, thinkeing by that meanes to make his owne peace, how should I aunswere it, that haue him now in my handes, and my lord's warraunt to make him sure? Againe what a Blemish would it be to all my actions, if the kinge, at his first Coming in, should finde all the kingdome quiet but onelie this litle parte vnder my Charge. This moued Mee [to send for him] Presentlie, & when hee came I tould him the Newes of the Queene's death. Hee seamed to be sorrie for it. I tould him of the Succession of the kinge, then ame I vndone sayeth hee, for Roory hath better freindes about him then I. That speach encreased my iealousie, & therevpon I tould him further I had order from my lord to restraine him of his libertie. Then ame I a dead man, saith hee. I tould him noe, hee needed not feare any such matter, neither his life nor landes were yet in danger, his offence was a Comtempte onelie, & hee must be brought to acknowledge a higher Power then his owne. The Marshall offerred to put Boults on him; hee sent vnto Mee & desired hee might not be handled with that indignitie, protesting with many oathes he would not offerr to flie away. I bad the Marshall forbeare, & hee desired then I would allowe him a guard of a dosen of Souldiers to looke to him, & soe I did. Then did hee seriouslie (as I thought) acknowledge his follye, promised faithfullie to doe nothing hereafter but by my Councell. I tould him if hee did soe, let him not fear, his Cryme was not Capitall, & that hee might well see by his vsage, for hee had libertie to walke vp & downe in the towne with his guard onelie. Hee seamed wounderfull thankfull for it, & my intentions were now wholie bent to doe him all the good offices might lye in my Power, but the third day after hee had beene thus Restrayned hee secreetlie caused a horse, to be brought to the towne gate, & noe man suspecting anythinge, hee sudainelie slipt aside & gott vp vpon him, & soe made an escape. Word being brought vnto Mee of it, I was then, I confess, extreamlie irritated against him, & castinge about what to doe, presentlie coniectured hee would goe to his Creaghtes, that lay about 8 Myle from the Liffer, & with him gett downe to the Bottome of Tyrconnell toward the Ilands, where I knewe was the greatest strenght he could goe to, & furthest (of any other) out of my reach. Therefore I sent first to Captaine Ralph Bingley that lay at Ramullan, fitt in the way to Cross his passage, that hee should speedilie make out to stoppe him till I came, which should be so soone as I could, & then to the Garrison att Liffer that they should follow him to whome Roory O'Donnell (being there at that time) readily wyned himselfe as glad of soe faire an opportunitie to advaunce his owne endes by. I was not deceiued in my Coniecture, & soe by that time I had writt these lettres, made ready the Souldiers to goe with Mee, was past ouer Lough Swilley by boate, & had marched some 7 or 8 Mile, I mett with the Newes that our Men had ouertaken & beate him, gott possession of the Cowes, which he fought for & defended with force of Armes as longe as hee was able (& were estimated to be about 7000,) & that hee himselfe was fledd into Mac Swyndoe's Countrey, with a purpose to gett into Owen Oge's Castle, which was reputed to be the strongest in all the North. I had then Owen Oge in my Companie, & to preuent him Required he would deliuer it to Mee, & soe hee did, onelie requesting hee might haue it againe, when the Garrison I should put in it, should be withdrawne, which I gaue my word vnto, hee should; & then seeing himselfe preuented of a place to retire vnto, spoyled of all his goods, & nothing in the world left him to liue vpon, hee sent vnto Mee for a Protection to goe safe vnto my lord Deputie, & takeing his Brother for his Pledge, & his oath besids, that he would goe & submitt himselfe wholie to his Judgement, I was contented & gaue it him, put the Pray wee had taken from him vpon Roory O'Donnell's hand, because hee should not haue that pretense to say I had driuen him out of purpose to make Prey of his goods, & soe promised to be there ere longe & meete him; for nowe I had receiued diuers lettres againe, one that my lord was purposed shortelie to goe for England, that his Maiestie (by his recommendation) was pleased to call Mee to be one of the

Councell of Ireland, & that hee would haue Mee to come speake with him before his departure; annother to Comaund mee to suffer the Earle of Tyrone's Men to retourne to theire landes, & especially to the Salmon fishing of Lough Foyle, which till this time I had enioyed, & was promised the inheritaunce of, as a parte of the reward for my seruice; And annother for restitution of Castles, Tennements, Catle, & many other thinges vnto him which altogeather gaue Mee occasion presentlie to prepaire my selfe to that iourney.

But first by the way, let the reader, if hee please, now enter into Consideration, & lay togeather before him, the some of all that which is written before, Imagining withall, he nowe sees A towne at the Derrey (for soe there was) built with litle or noe Charge to the Queene, able, besids the houses, for stowage of Munition & victuell sent by the state, to lodge convenientlie (in those erected by our owne labour & industrie onelie) a 1000 Men with theire officers; Hee shall see besids where wee landed on the 16th of May 1600, & found not soe much as a drie sticke to succor our selues, with or vnder, the rest of the Countrey abounding with howses, Corne, Catle, & a People that had beene bredd vpp in Armes, flusht with former victories, & inrictched with the spoile of the rest of the kingdome; Now, that parte wee held onely replenished with such Corne & Catle as was left, the People reclaymed to obedience, quiett & safe vnder our protection, & the rest desolute & waste, the People vpon it brought to desperate Extremitie, and enioying nothing but as fugitiues, & what they troad vpon by stealth; let him alsoe Consider what Castles & places of strength I haue gott & maintayned, noe one of them lost againe for want of victuelling, or other prouident care, noe disgrace taken by the Armye, nor soe much as a parte of it at any time beaten in the field: And when last of all, that nowe on the 24th of March 1602 (for on that day was Tyrone taken in) the bussines done that wee came for, & the Warre happilie & gloriouslie ended; And as annother, writing a discourse vpon the Battaile of Kinsaile, where my lord worthylie gayned himselfe Eternall honnor (and yet had his actions depraued as well as I myne) tooke occasion to make Comparison of the state of the kingdome as it then was, with that it was at his first Cominge, & said of it (in his behalfe) as one argument for all against Enuious & detracting tongues, *Quantum mutatus ab illo*; May not I from that I found it in (without flattery to myselfe or vaine ostentation) say as much of the state of this parte of it Committed to my charge. Let

Mallice accuse mee if I haue spoken vntruth, & then I refuse not the Judgement of any that is Ingenious.

I could speake of a greate many more workes that we did, whereof the Countrey can not but afford a Memory to this day: But my intent was from the begininge to touch onely the principall thinges, & noe more.

And soe to retourne where I left, my intent of going to Dublin being publiquely knowne, diuers came to Mee with seuerall Requests & Remembrances; and first O'Caine, who tould Mee the Earle of Tyrone had sent some Men of his to be Cessed vpon him, which did intimate as if hee were made Lord of his Countrey, woundred at it, because if it were soe, it was directlie against my lord's Promise, & therefore desired Mee to make his excuse that he receiued them not.

Then O Doughertie, that he heard my lord went to giue away the Ile of Inch from him, & appealed to Mee that it was against the agreement made betweene vs.

Younge Tirlough, sonne to Sir Arthur ONeale, that my lord had alreadie giuen order for the deliuery of Newtowne into my lord of Tyrone's hand, challenged Mee of my Promise, & further desired his father's lands might be assigned him. My Guides & spyes, such as I had made many vses of, that the warres nowe ended, they might be restored to the landes they had formerlie dwelt vpon, & be saued [saved] from the Mallice of my lord of Tyrone & others that held them a deadly hatred, onelie for the seruice they had done vnto vs.

The sonne of one of them alsoe Complayned, that presentlie soe soone as the peace was published, his father going into Tyrone, to vissitt & make merrey with some of his old acquaintaunce, was taken vp & hanged by my lord of Tyrone's express Comaundement, & telling mee whoe they were that ffrst laid handes on him, I sente and apprehended them, tooke theire Examinations & kepte them in Prison.

Somewhat I had to say for myselfe, & a greate deale about Neale Garvie, & with theire Memorialls to speak of when I came there, I sett forward my intended iourney, & when I came to my lord's presence, I found him (as I thought) exceeding fauorable, & well affected towards Mee, for which after I had made profession of due & humble thankes, soe soone as the time serued fitly for it, wee entred into speach.

Ffirst, of Neale Garvie, whoe was there present Busyly framing Complaints against mee, whome my lord reiected, & would not

vouchsafe to say any more vnto but onelie this: Neale Garuye, yow ae
greatlie indebted vnto the state, for the entertainements yow haue had
& done litle for, I haue often heard yow Complayned of for many ill
Conditions, & now by my owne Experience, I finde it hath not been
without iust cause, & therefore yow shall not expect any further fauour from mee, but be assured of seueritie according to your deserts.
Hee beganne to replye, but my lord would not giue him the hearing.
Then his lordship & I fell to in talke of him betweene our selues, and
first he protested touching Roory O'Donell, that hee tooke him in
vpon a free and absolute submission, & letting him first knowe hee
had promised the Countrey of Tyrconell to another, soe that it lay not
in his Power to giue him soe much as a hope of any parte of it, so carefull he was of doing noe wronge to Neale Garuye, Neuertheless he was
not then Ignorant of his perverse behauiour, hee had warned him
often, sawe noe hope of amendment, & therefore was now fullie resolued to beare with him noe longer, but thought himselfe both in
honnor & Conscience free from all former Promises made vnto him;
I replyed, & wee had much speach about it; The some of all I saide
was this, that I could not say any thinge in his behalfe, I had soe often
Complayned of him before, nor had reason to doe it, in that I sawe
him senceless of his owne faults, & indevoring all hee could, to lay the
blaime of it vpon Mee ; yet many good seruices I neuer did, nor could
denie but hee had done, it was true, they were made vnsauorie by a
peruerse kinde of Carriage in him, which (I confess) I sawe noe hope
of amendment of, & certainelie his occasions made it manifest, he
affected not onelie a Soueraigne, but euen with all a tyrannycall power
ouer the landes & lyves & goodes of those people should liue in any
parte of the Countrey he accompted his, that this I had alwayes
opposed against, & from hence grewe all the Contentions that were
betweene vs; That he had verified all I had euer accused him of, by his
late disobedience to his lordship's owne Comaunde, & violentlie
assuming to himselfe, that which hee might not haue done but by
aucthoritie from annother; that in his heart I was verylie perswaded
hee was at this time a Malitious Rebbell, & if it might be done with
iustice, the safest course were to take of his heade, but if he had not
done anythinges that Lawe could take hould of in that kinde, I sawe
not how his lordship could thinke himselfe freed of his Promises, nor
what other punishment could be inflicted vpon him, but such as was
due for a high Contempte, & that vndoubtedlie he was most worthie

of: But if hee intended to giue away his whole Countrey from him to annother, besides the apparent breach of his Promise, there would many inconveniences insue of it, if hee divided it in any fashion whatsoeuer, he should but sowe the seeds of ciuill discention, soe as to say truth, what meane course might be had with him was a difficulte point to resolue on; But whatsoeuer his lordship would please to doe in it, I wisht hee might haue a Publique hearing & a Judiciall Sentence pronounced vpon him, other wayes I sawe noe way possible to giue any Colour of satisfaction to the World. In the end our Conclusion was this; Hee badd Mee bethinke myselfe, & sett downe in writing the vttermost of what I could charge him withall, & the proofes I was able to make, & to send it after him into England, & there hee would resolue to proceed with him accordinglie: I did soe, & spared not any thing I could speake with truth against him, as hauing my heart inclyned at that time to doe him noe fauour; I sent it by Captaine Harte, togeather with a discourse about O'Caine, both it & my lettres written both at that & other times into whose hands soeuer they are fallen, will giue a full testimoniall of truth to all this which I now say; but it wrought other effects then I either intended or expected.

Then touching O'Caine I tould him [Lord Mountjoy] how the Earle of Tyrone had sent men to be cessed vpon him, & how hee refused them; Sr Henry Docwra sayeth hee; My lord of Tyrone is taken in with promise to be restored, aswell to all his lands, as his honnor of Dignitie, & O'Caine's Countrey is his, & must be obedient to his Comaund. My lord, said I, this is strange & beyond all expectation, for I ame sure your lordship cannot be vnmindfull, first of the agreement I made with him, wherein he was promised to be free & to hould his lands from the Crowne, & then your lordship ratified & approued the same vnto him vnder your hand, haue iterated it againe diuers & diuers times both by word of Mouth & writing, how shall I looke this man in the face when I shall knowe myselfe guilty directlie to haue falsified my word with him; Hee is but a drunken ffellowe saith hee, and soe base, that I doe not thinke but in the secreete of his hearte, it will better Content him to be soe then otherwise, besides hee is able neither to doe good nor hurte, & wee must haue a Care to the Publique good, & giue Contentment to my lord of Tyrone, vpon which depends the Peace & securitie of the whole kingdome. My Lord, said I, for his drunkenness & disabillitie to doe good or hurte, they are not heere to come into Consideration, & for his inward affections, what they are I know not, But sure I ame hee makes outward shewe, that this will be very displeasing vnto him, and the manifest, & manifould benifitts hee shall receiue more by the one then the other, are to my vnderstanding sufficient arguments to make mee thinke hee doth seriouslie inclyne to his owne good, & with your fauour, what good can ensue to the Publique by a direct breach of Promise whereof there is soe plaine vndeniable Evidence extante vnder our hands, it passeth my vnderstanding to Conceiue. Well sayeth hee againe, that I haue done was not without the aduise of the Councell of this kingdome, it was liked of & approued by the lords in England, by the Queene that is deade, & by the king's Maiestie that is now liv-ing, & I ame perswaded not without good & sufficient Reason; It may not be infringed, but if yow can thinke vpon any course to Compasse it in some good fashion that I be troubled noe more with it, I shall take it as an acceptable kindnes; But howsoeuer, By God, sayeth hee, O'Cane must & shall be vnder my lord Tyrone. I then tould him I had noe more to say, though I were not soe fullie satisfied as I could wish; yet hee should see my will was, & should be obedient & Conformeable to his, let it be soe, sayeth hee, & you shall doe mee a pleasure.

Then touching O'Doughertie I tould him hee had hard his lordship had a purpose to giue away the Ile of Inche from him, which hee had shewed Me was expreslie contayned in this father's Graunte, & there-fore would importe a breach of Promise both of myne & his owne; Hee acknowledged he had beene moued in such a matter, but thanked mee for telling him thus much & bad mee be assured it should not be done, wherewith I rested fullie satisfied & tould O'Doughertie as much, whoe was at that time in towne in my Compaine.

Then I came to younge Tirlough & tould him I had receiued a gen-erall Warraunt from his lordship to restore all the Castles & houlders that I had in Tyrone, into my lord's hands That there were two videlicet the Castle of Newtowne & Dongevin, that were deliuered to Mee vpon Condition, that the Kinge hauing noe longer vse of them, they should haue them againe from whome I receiued them, & besids that of Newtone was parte of the peculier lands belonging to Sir Arthur O'Neale, whose sonnes there were very many reasons for, should be fauored & respected by the state; Hee tould Mee it was with him as it was with O'Caine all that Countrey was my lord of Tyrone's & what hee might be intreated to giue him, he might haue, But otherwise he could challeng noe right nor intrest in anythinge, & therefore for the Castles badd mee againe deliuer them, & for younge Tirlough, hee would speake to my lord (of Tyrone) to deale well with him. ffor my Guids & Spyes I then saw my aunswere before hand, & that it was bootleless to Motion for any landes for them, yet I tould him what seruices many of them had done, what promises I had made them how vtterlie destitute of meanes they were to liue vpon, & how much I thought the state was ingaged both in honnor and Pollicie to prouide for & protect them; Hee said he would speake to my lord of Tyrone in theire behalfe, & badd mee giue them what I thought good in victuells out of the kings stoore, & it should be allowed of; I was somewhat importunate for a Certaintie & Countynuance of meanes for them to liue vpon & that by aucthoritie of the state, they might be allowed to retourne to theire owne landes. But he would not indure to heare of it; yet hee spake to my lord of Tyrone in my presence, and he promised freelie to forgiue all that was past, & to deale with them as kindlie as with the rest of his Tenants; howbeit afterwardes I could giue particuler instance wherein he changed his Note and Sunge annother tune.

I theu tould him of my Guide that my lord of Tyrone had hanged, he aunswered, he thought it was not without some iust cause, I desired that cause might be knowne, & the matter come to open tryall; Hee seemed to be extreamelie offended to be troubled with Complaints of that kinde, & my lorde of Tyrone said for his excuse, my lord had giuen him aucthoritie to execute Martiall lawe, & this was a knaue taken robbinge a Priest, & therefore worthyly put to Death. I was able to proue the Contrary, & offerred to doe it vpon perill of my life, by the Confessions of those Men I had at that time Prisoners in my hand; But seeing the Bussines soe displeasing to my lord I gaue it ouer, & afterwards one of them that was cheife in the action breaking Prison, I sett the rest at libertie.

Then came I lastlie to my selfe, & tould him I receiued order from him to suffer the Earle of Tyrone's men to fish the Riuer of Loughfoyle, I hoped his lordship had not forgott, that hitherto hee had giuen Mee the proffitts of it & promised mee the inheritaunce & that it was not his meaning to take if from Mee againe; Hee said Sr Henry Docwra, yow haue deserued well of the kinge, & your seruice, there is greate Reason should be Recompenced, But it must be by some other meanes then this. Yow see what promise I haue made to my lord of Tyrone, & it is not my Priuate affection to any man living that shall make mee breake it, because I knowe it is for the Publique good; yow must therefore let him haue both that & the lands which were reserued from O'Caine and on my honnor, yow shall be otherwise worthylie rewarded. I expected nothing less then such an answere, yet I made noe further wordes, But willinglie yealded to giue vp my intrust in both & departed at that time aswell contented without them, as I should haue beene glad to haue had them. Then I desired to haue gone with him into England, but he would not suffer Mee; But with exceeding fauorable Countenance assured mee to do me all right vnto the kinge; & soe was I satisified with hopes, though any man may see I had hitherto nothing bettered my selfe by this Journey.

As he was readie to take shipping, O'Doghertie came & tould Mee, that notwithstanding all the assurance I had giuen him of the Contrary, the Ile of Inch was past away. I could not possiblie belieue it at first, but hee showed mee manifest proofes that a lease was graunted for XXI years; I then badd him goe speake for himselfe, for I had done as much as I was able, wherevpon hee followed him into England and had such reamidie as shall presently be declared.

In the meane time being gone, my lord Hugh (the Earle of Tyrone's eldest sonne) & I went home togeather, & when wee came to to the Derrey, I sent for O'Caine, & tould him what my lords pleasure was touchinge him; Hee beganne presentlie to be moued, & both by Speach & gesture, declared as earnestlie as was possible, to be highlie offended at it, argued the matter with Mee vpon many pointes protested his fidelitie to the state since hee had made profession of it; asked noe fauour if any man could charge him with the Contrarie, said he had alwayes buylt vpon my promise & my lord Deputie's, that he was nowe vndone, & in worse case then before hee knewe vs, shewed many reasons for it, & asked, if wee would Claime him hereafter, if hee followed my lord of Tyrone's Councell though it were against the kinge, seeing hee was in this manner forced to be vnder him; In the end seeing noe remidie, hee shaked handes with my lord Hugh, bad the Devill take all English Men & as many as put theire trust in them, & soe in the shewe of a good reconciled frenshipp they went away togeather.

I was then to write vnto my lord of many other thinges, & thought this no impertinent matter to lett him knowe of, yet with a

Protestation, neuer to open my mouth in it more. Captaine Heart who is yet liuing carried that dispatch, & tould Mee when hee came backe againe hee thought I had offended him in somewhat in those lettres, for he gathered as much from his Countenance, when hee read them, & besides he found him nothinge fauorable to anythinge he had occasion to speake vnto him of in my behalfe; But my hearte was soe Cleere & soe Confident of him at that time, that I could not possiblie beleeue it.

Within a while after came Roory O'Donnell to Dublin, with his Maiestie's lettres to be made Earle of Tirconnell, & haue all the Countrey to him & his heires (except Ballyshannon with 1000 acres of ground & the fishing that lyes vnder it) & such landes as Neale Garvie had held; living in amitie with the former O'Donell, the said Neale garuie iudiciallie convicted of noe Crime which I thought was strange, But whither it were with his right or wronge with Conveniencie or inconveniencie to the state, was then noe more to be disputed of. Hee brought a warraunt alsoe to haue Owen Oge's Castle deliuered vnto him, which because of my Promise I opposed against as much as I could but with lost labour.

Presentlie after him came O'Doghertie alsoe with a lettre from my lord to Mee, to pray mee to deliuer him the possession of the Ile of Inch againe, which hee himselfe had past away before, first by lease for XXI yeares, & afterwardes in ffee simple for euer, both vnder the greate seale; I tould him this warraunt was too weake to doe what it imported, & shew'd him reasons for it, which either he could not, or would not, apprehend, or beleeue, But plainely made shew to conceiue a suspition as though I were corrupted vnder hand to runne a dissembleing course with him. To giue him Contentment if I could, being then to goe for England, & to Dublin by the way, I spoke to Sr. George Carey that was then lord Deputie, tould him how the case stoode, & what discontentment I sawe it draue him into. Hee tould Mee it was past the Seales (gaue mee a further reason too) & vtterlie refused to make or medle with it; Herevpon hee tooke it more to hearte, sente Agentes to deale for him in England, they preuayled not till my lord was deade, & then with impatience lead away with Lewd Councell besides, & conceiuing himselfe to be wronged in many other thinges, hee was first brooke out into open Rebbellion, but that fell out a good while after.

In the meane time I went forward my Journey, & Coming to my

lord to the Coute, propounded in my owne private bussines, to haue
a booke of 100 towne land in Ireland as others had gotten both before
& after Mee, it was allowed of & vndertaken at first; But within fewe
dayes after I was told it could not be obtayned; Then desired I might
haue the Gouernement of Loughfoyle, with the Entertaynement of
20's a daye established to mee during life which I had alreadie by the
king's lettres pattents but during pleasure & the towne I had built at
the Derrey, if it might be thought fitt (not for any gayne of myne) to
be incorporate & haue such Priuiliges as might be thought reasonable
& convenient for it.

This without difficultie I was promised should be done; But coming to Sr. Thomas Wyndebancke to whome I was referred for my dispatch, I found order for my entertainement, with my aucthoritie, &
gouernement restrayned onely to the towne; This I disliked of & went
to my lord nothing doubting but to haue it redressed: But hee tould
mee it was the king's pleasure noe man should haue to doe in my lord
of Tyrones Countrey, and before I could make replie, turned away, &
would not vouchsafe Mee and further Speach. There was nothing
could fall vnto Mee so farre beyond expectation, as this strange & soddaine alienation of his Countenance from Mee. I Sought first by
myselfe to knowe the reason of it, & none would be giuen, I vsed the
intercession of freindes, a pretence was intimated, & I cleered my selfe
of it with his owne acknowledgement to be fullie satisfied. Then hee
gaue mee the testimoney to be a worthie & honnest Gentleman, &
well deseruing for my seruice, But his priuate affections must in this
case giue way to the publique good, & beside, that soe it must be, was
his Maiestie's pleasure, I replyed againe how Ignomynious it would be
vnto Mee, & what an vnprofitable Journey I should make to retourne
in worse case then I came forth, some reasonable good wordes I had
in the end to encourage Mee to haue a hope of better Conditions
hereafter, but for the present I must be contented, there was noe possible remedie, soe after Six Monethes attendance, his Maiestie's lettres
I had for Confirmation of my Entertaynement onelie, and incorpo-
rating the towne vnder the Gouernement of a Prouost, which I was
named to be (with power to make a vice Prouost in my absence) during my life. And here is the Reward I haue had to this day for my 21
yeares' seruice in the Warres before, my aucthoritie & Countenance
one halfe dyminished, the fishing of Loughfoyle taken away, & the
land reserued from O'Caine. My lord Danuers yet liues & was well

acquainted with all that past betweene him & Mee, att this time, a knowne freinde of his & therefore a witnes free from all Exception. I will not press him to say all that hee knowes, But as hee is honnorable, I appeale to his Testimonye, whether all this that I say be not true, & that if I listed I could say much more to myne owne aduantage, which I willinglie pass ouer, & cann be well enough Contented shalbe buried in eternall sylence.

But takeing my leaue at Courte, & departing with this dispatch for Ireland, the windes as I went put mee in at Knockfergus & my lord Deputie that nowe is, being then Gouernor of that place, & established in it by Pattent during his life, was the first that asked mee, if I were not discharged of my Gouernement. I tould him noe; hee presentlie shewed mee the Coppie of a lettre that my lord of Tyrone had sent vnto him, the orriginall whereof he had receiued from my lord Leiuetentant, declaring & giuing notice vnto him, that it was his Maiestie's Pleasure I should haue noe more to doe in his Countrey. wherevpon I tould him the whole truth, which hee seemed to wounder att & euen then to conceiue to be an Iniurie done vnto Mee. And passing by land from thence to the Derrey, I found the same Copies in euery man's hands all alonge as I went, & soe both my Comission (& estimation withall) publiquely decryed, for from that day forward the people amongst whome I had before as much loue as I thinke, as much respect I ame sure, as any man of my rancke in the Kingdome, beganne to Contemne mee with as many Skornes & affronntes, as the witt & malice of any that hated Mee could desire, or listed to putt into theire heades to doe Mee.

Not long after himselfe coming to receiue the Sword, & foreseeing the bussines, that would arise from those partes could not but necessarilie require some man of aucthoritie to be resident amongst them, & bearing a noble & speciall respect vnto me withall, badd Mee for any inhibition I had yet receiued, I should not be Scrupulous, but freelie take vpon Mee the execution of my Comission. I tould him it would be offensiue to my lord. Hee tooke vpon himselfe to beare the blame of it, & see, by vertue of his Comaunde, & yet not without further expresse warraunt & direction besides, some thinges I did, but they were presentlie Complayned of, and my lord wrote vnto him to dissist, And where before, the restraint lay onelie vpon Tyrone, hee now lay the like vpon Tyrconell alsoe, & sent him warraunt to make the Earle Justice of Peace & Quorum, & lord Lieuetenant of that

Countrey; How much to the preiudice of those that had faithfully
serued the state, I could, if it were required euen at this day, giue many
particuler instances and proofes of, & take occasion further to make
longe discourses vpon this man's violent and insolent Carriage, sufficiently bewraying to any man that listed to see it, what the bent of his
heart was from the begining; But hee is deade, & the iniuryes that
honnest Men receiued by him are past Recouerie, & therefore I will
onelie say this of him in gennerall wordes (& I thinke my lord
Deputie & Judges that were in that time, will beare mee witnes I say
true) there were noe vices in poore Neale Garvie, that had done vs
many good seruices, But the same were in him, & more, in a farre
more pernitious degree, that had neuer done any, & then I Confess it
made mee see cleere myne owne Errour, & the wronge (I may call it)
I had done to Neale Garvye; not that my Conscience accuseth mee to
haue done any thinge towards him with malitious or corrupt intentions (noe thereof I take God to witnes my heart is cleere) But that
with Simplicitie I suffered my selfe to be made an Instrument of his
ouerthrowe, vnder the pretence of those misbeheauors, that were
plainelie tollerated yea & allowed of in another, ffor it is true my lord
would heare noe Complainte of him howe iust soeuer.

And to giue me a further testimonye of what I might hope for at his
handes, Ballyshannon being taken by mee in manner as before is mentioned, hee made Sr Henry Ffollyott Gouernour of it by pattent during his life, laid 1000 acres of land to the Castle, & gaue him the
inheritaunce of the fyshinge, noe Consideration of offending the Irish,
& by Consequence of inconvenience to the Publique, which were euer
the pretended impediments to all my demaundes, any wayes with-
standinge; yea & to some other of inferiour Ranckes to myselfe, he
gaue large Proportion of landes, parte whereof, as that from
O'Doughertie in perticuler was with a direct breach of promise and
Couenant, both of myne & his owne, where neither for myselfe, nor
the Towne of Derrey, nor by way of Reward for any Captaine that
serued vnder Mee (by any suite or meanes I could make) could I gett
so much as one foot, of that which without iniurie to any man living,
and with great Convenience to the king's seruice (as I ame perswaded)
hee might haue giuen if hee had pleasd.

All this & much more (though very irksome it was) I indured & sitt
out withall a yeare & better; In the end tyred with the exercise of
Pacience, & not without iust cause (as I can make it plainelie appeare

to any man that desires to be satisfied in that pointe) dispareing of my safetie to liue any longer in place, I came away for England, & adressed myselfe both to him & others, that I thought might & would haue giuen or procured mee better Conditions; But they tould Mee the kinge had put all into his handes, & hee, the old songe, it was for the good of the Publique; And then seeing noe meanes I could make able to preuaile (after at least 4 Monethes tryall) I came & tould him to this effect, There was noe death could be soe bitter to Mee as the life was I had ledd, since I receiued these arguments of his disfauour, I was neither willing nor able to contest against him, & had therefore resolued though with a greate deale of greife of mind, & apparent loss of all my former laboures, to quitt myselfe of Ireland, & retourne noe more vnto it, was minded to sell away my house, & some lands I purchased there, & besought him to giue mee leaue to doe away my Companyes (that I yet held in the King's pay) togeather with them; Hee demaunded whoe it was I ment them vnto, I tould him Mr. George Pawlett a Gentleman of Hampshire, hee said hee knewe the man well, there was noe longer vse for a Man of warre in that place, & with a good will I should haue his Consente vnto it; I had not in truth at that time, past any such absolute promise to Mr. Pawlett, But perceiuing by this his willingnes to be ridd of Mee, & vrged vpon it shortelie after by some that were powerfull in fauour about him, to dispatch & goe forward with myne offer, takeing that as a Manifest argument aboue all the rest, what the secreet intentions of his hearte were towards Mee, I concluded a bargaine, & sold him my house I had builte, with 10 Quarters of land I had bought & layde to it (all with myne owne Money) & my Company of foote all togeather, for less a greate deale then the very house alone had stood mee in, & withall, the vice provostshipp of the towne of Derrey (for the time of my absence) I conferred vpon him, but which, I neither valued nor had anythinge for, And my Company of horse a good while after, by the fauour and allowance of the lordes of the Councell, I made ouer to my Leiuetenant; But aucthoritie ouer the Countrey, which I myselfe was discharged of, it lay not in my power to giue or sell, neither did I promise nor intend vnto him as my lord Deputie well knowes, & the Counterpaynes of writinges that past betweene vs are able to testifie vnto this day; ffor that onelie was it, which might I haue enioyed vpon any Reasonable or indifferent tearmes I take it vpon my Saluation, It was not 5 times the money I had for all the rest, should haue bought mee out of it; And that therein I should desire to haue Contynued, being none other but the same, I had brought the Countrey to obedience by from the height of Rebellion, & that which my Reputation & safetie of living in that place depended vpon, was not (as I take it) an ambitious affecting of all, as it pleased my lord to tearme it; And lett the pretence be what it will, that it might not haue beene with the Convenience to the kings Seruice aswell in mee as in others, that were in the same case, noe one in the kingdome hauing the like Restrainte laide vpon him, but onely I, was a Paradox I confess, beyond my Capassitie to beleeue, & I ame sure the after events plentifullie proued to be a false one.

And now because O'Caine, from the breach of my promise with him, deriues, aswell, as he may, the cause of all his Miseries, & therevpon (as he sayeth) hath often made suite to haue a day of hearing at the Councell table, & diuers times importuned Mee to be present at it, & my aunswere hath alwayes beene, lett mee be called & asked, I would not spare to speake the full of the truth according to my knowledg; But for soe doing, neither hee nor I haue hitherto had any such opportunitie; To satisfie my Conscience in that pointe, by makeing it knowne (as much as lyeth in my Power) what the true state of his case is, I doe now averre, all that I haue said alreadie concerning him is true, & further, that while I was yet in Ireland, there were some that came & perswaded him, howsoeuer either my Creditt, or will, fayled to doe him right, they would vndertake to make my agreement with him good by lawe, & that if hee would, they would procure him his landes to himselfe; Hee came to Mee vpon it, & asked my advise, I bad him giue noe creditt vnto them, they would not be able to prevaile against my lord Leiuetenant, & hee would be brought into worse case, then yet he was, if hee shewed himselfe refractory against my lord of Tyrone, & therefore wished him to bende himselfe rather to seeke his fauour, & stirre noe further in it, yet others after that came againe & endeuored to instill into him the same hopes, with such vehement & forcible perswations, that in the end he beganne to inclyne & giue eare vnto them. Tyrone perceyving it, & iealous of the event, labored as much on the contrary side, both by arguments of reason and Promises of fauours, to binde him the faster to himselfe, & still bad him gett before his Eyes, the fruits of his trust to any Promises of ours, by the Examples of his forepast Experience, & because hee sawe the greatest argument that swayd him from his side, was an obiection, that in the state he now was, hee had neither lands nor goods of his owne, but for both stood meerelie at the Courtesie of annother, to take away that feare, hee made him a Graunte of his owne landes to him & his heires for euer, at a certaine Rente in writing vnder his hand, & therevpon (as the Fame went) he resolutely vowed his fidelitie to him; And then came I away, & what was done in the Progress, & after Carriage of that bussines, I ame not able to speake of my owne certaine knowledge, more then onelie this, that Questions arisinge betweene them againe, & both of them called to the Councell table at Dublin, to haue them debated, I ame sure O'Cane produced that writinge to shew in Evidennce, & Tyrone laide hould on it, & before the Deputie & all the rest of theire faces tore it in Peces. If all this notwithstanding hee were afterwardes Guiltie of any disloyaltie to the kinge It is more than any man charged him of in my time, & it belonges not to Mee, therein to excuse or extenuate his faulte, lett him aunswere for himselfe.

And because in the begining of this discourse, I sett downe the list of the Army, to be frist 4000 foote, & 200 horse, then by the Casting of Sr. Mathew Morgan's Regiament, that he foote were brought to 3000, & afterwardes I mention Supplyes, but speake nothinge of further abatements, whereby the Reader may probably Conceiue as though the lyst had contynued at that rate, & thereby I should wronge myselfe, I thought it fitt to say thus much more, that although I cannot call to Minde euery particuler abatement when it was made, yet diuers there were contynuallie from time to time, & at least 3 Monethes before the Warre ended, I ame sure I had not left Mee in list aboue 1000 foote & 50 horse at the most.

And thus haue I nowe gone thorough (with as much breuitie as I cann) to declare to the veiwe of those, that shall please to see it, the true state of the Bussines betweene my lord & Mee. It is not enough perhappes to some that will yet thinke all this insufficient to excuse Mee for quitting myselfe from the king's Seruice, & may obiecte, further, why did I not address myselfe vnto him: hee was gratious, & wise, & whatsoeuer I had found his pleasure to bee, was both a sufficient lawe to binde Mee, & a reason to giue me Contentment; It is true euen wisemen some times comitt Errours, & none but arrogant fooles presume to iustifie them when they are done; as I ame not the one, soe I would not be the other, & therefore I do herein willinglie & Sincerelie acknowledge my faults, & yet with truth haue thus much to say in my Excuse, without mediation of freindes it could not be done, & they on whose fauours I had (as I thought) some Reason to Relye ( because of my anciente Dependaunce vpon them) refused mee, & to seeke it by newe acquaintaunce, I had Considerations (not vnworthie to enter into an honnest Man's thoughts) that discouraged Mee; Besids I must freelie confess the contemplation of his power & height in fauour dazled myne Eyes, & greife & indignation did litle less then putt them Cleene out; yea & further I should wronge myselfe if I did denye, but that some Meditations I had in hand to take Course Safe, & Justifiable in all Respects, If not to haue righted my selfe by, yet at least to have manifested both my wronges & myne inocency to Publique knowledge, which whatsoeuer it was, his suddaine & vnexpected Death preuented, & by occasion thereof, I haue since had leasure too much to bethinke my Selfe of my follie, & meanes too litle to putt my Selfe into any way to redress it; The onelie Reamidie I desire, is to be admitted againe to his Maiestie's Service, & therein to Spende my dayes, is the height of happines, that I aspire vnto, & to bringe Mee vnto it, shall be the Worke of him, that worthely and eternally, shall binde my affections of love & fidelitie vnto him; Artificiall, or florishing wordes to insinuate my selfe into fauour by, I neither affect, nor Nature hath bestowed the giuft on Mee to vse; But I profess to haue a true & faithfull Hearte, & yett, if the Course of my life haue at any time told the Contrary, my Profession is vaine, & I haue done, lett noe man beleeue Mee.

FINIS.

# REMARKS ON THE PRECEDING TRACT

THE foregoing tract is printed from a MS copy which is evidently of an age contemporaneous with the writer, now preserved in the Library of the Irish Ordnance Survey Office, Mountjoy Barracks, Phoenix Park, Dublin. It is in a plain strong clerk hand, and the fly-leaf exhibits the autograph of "Theodore Docwra," but no date. The original, in Sir Henry Docwra's own hand, is said to be in the posses-sion of Sir Thomas Phillipps, Bart, of Middle Hill, who has not con-descended to communicate to the Society any account of the state of the MS. The probability is that the original consists of rough notes and various original letters, which were drawn up into the following form by a professional scribe under Sir Henry Docwra's own direction, and that the present copy in the Ordnance Survey Library was made for the use of Theodare Docwra, the son and heir of the author.

There are various Genealogical memoranda, and Armorial bearings of several branches of the Docwra's family, as of Cambridge, Yorkshire, Herts, &c. preserved in the Library of the British Museum, (Egerton, No. 74, 6769, &c.) but the descent of our author does not appear among them. In March, 1599, he was appointed by letters patent under the great seal of the Realm, "Chief Commander and Governor of all her Majesty's forces of horse and foot assigned for Lough Foyle." And in the same month the following instructions were given to him and Sir Matthew Morgan from her Majesty's Castle of Dublin by the Lord Deputy and Council.

*Bibl. Lambeth, No. 632, fol. 189*

Instructions gyven by vs the *Lorde Deputie* and Councell to our trustie and well-beloved Sir Henrie Dockwraye, Knight, appointed Cheefe Commander and governor of all her majesties forces of horse and foote assigned for Loughfoile, and the parts mentioned and limited in her Majestie's Letters Pattents, vnder the great Seale of this Realme made to him, and dated Martij 1599, in the 42 yere of Her Majestie's raigne.

Ffirst Consideringe the principall foundation of all good goverment restethe in the due service of Allmightie God, after yow haue settled your self and Companies in the place where yow are to reside, yow shall before all other things provide that your Preacher appointed to yow for that purpose, maye be dilligent in his Chardge to instruct and teach all those that are vnder your rule in the trewe vnderstandinge of God's holie woorde, and to laboure to beate downe amongst them all vice, as swearinge, Adultery, fornication, vnlawfull playinge at dice and Cardes, with all other impieties and blas-phemies, hatefull to good Christians, and most daungerous to be suffered with impunnitie in Armies, or amongst any other Christian Congregation or soesieties of men.

And next for that the second grownde of good goverment resteth vppon administration of Civall Justice, yow are to take Care to see that Justice be distributed sincearely and vprightlie amongst those that are vnder your Chardge, aswell Englishe as Irishe, and not for favoure or other respects to breake the lawes and rewles thereof, whereby yow shall the better leade the Troopes vnder your Chardge, in obedience to God and her Majestie, and in dutie and love towards your self.

And for that the troopes of Horse and foote assigned for that service, and Committed to your rule and gouerment, is the strenngth that yow are to repose in, yt is requisit that yow be verye Carefull to haue all the Companies Compleat in nvmbers of men and armes, And all other furnitures fitt for ser-vice, and to that ende yow are to see that frequent and exact musters be taken of the severall Companies by the Commissary appointed for that purpose, whome yow are to direct and Commaunde to performe the dutie of his place without partiallitie or affection, but faithefully and sincerely as becometh an officer of soe greate truste, and aboue all things to see that the fraude hereto-fore vsed in mosters, bothe to the robbinge of her Majestie in her purse, and shamefull abusinge of the service, may be reformed by his dilligence, and your ouersight of him.

Where it hathe pleased her Majestie out of her Princely disposition to allowe that an Hospitall for sicke and hurte Souldiours shalbe errected there in such apte and fitt place as to yow in discrescion shalbe thought meete, and hathe sent out of Englande good store of provisions and necessaries requisit for the same, That in any wise with the first Convenient opportunitye yow shall haue yow goe about the building of it, and to see it accommendated and well vsed accordinge her Majesties Royall meaninge therein. And as yow are to see the sicke, maymed, and hurte Souldiours to be succored & Comforted by this Howse duringe theire malledies and infirmityes soe on the other side yow are to foresee that noe Souldiour be suffered to remaine longer in the Hospitall then he is trewlie sicke or hurte, but beinge throughelie recouered to be retorned to his place, and in any wise not suffer any person that

Counterfetteth himself to be sicke or hurte to be admitted, into the Howse whereby to take the Comfort and benefitt of the Howse from others that are Justlie to be releeved with the same.

Whereby your letters Pattents vnder the great Seale yow haue Aucthoritie to prosequit with fyer and sworde all Rebbells and Traitours and other malle-factours and offendors within the lymit of your Commissions which will require greate advise foresight and Councell. Yow are therefore vpon anie greate occasion of service to Calle to yow soe many of the fathefull and best experienced Captaines and officers in your whole regiment, as yow thinke most meete to Conferre withall, and by waie of theire assistance as a Councell at warre to heere theire seuerall oppinions throwly to thende yow maye make Choise of them which shalbe thaught most meete for her majesties Service.

Where there are Certaine Shipps called Crompsters with other barkes and bardges, assigned for that service of Loughefoile, yow are to Communicat with the Captaines, Commaunders, maiesters, and other principall officers thereof. In what sorte Crompsters, barques, and barges maye be employed for the most advantadge of Her Maiestie's service, and therevppon to give them direction from tyme to tyme, vppon every good occasion that yow shall thinke meete, for which purpose the Captaines, Commaunders, maiesters, and pilatts of the said vessells are to be commaunded and disposed by yow and your aucthoritie.

Towchinge the victualls appointed and to be appointed for that service, there is a speciall Commissarie, John Travers gent assigned for that purpose, aswell to receave it into his Chardge and to see it well vsed preserved as much as maye be, as allsoe to see it dulie yssue to the Companies accordinge to the rates vsuall to the resedue of her majesties Armie in Irelande, and the Comissarie to keepe a perfect booke of the yssues of the victualls to the ende the same beinge trewlie Certified vnder his hande iuste and trewe defalcation maye be made accordingely. And towchinge the particuler rates the Commisarie hathe benne made acquainted with them heere by vs, besides his knowledge by the practize and employment he hathe had in that Kinde heere for which and for the particuler Issuinge of vittells vpon occasions to some ofthe Irish whome yow maye take in for Cause of service. The Comissarie doth bringe with him the Coppie of an Acte of Councell made heere to war-rant such issuinge soe as it passe by your direction vnder your hande.

Touching the powder and all such store of other munitions and Armes assigned and to be assigned for this service, yow are first to take a vewe of the generall quantities and howe much there is of every particuler kinde to the endeyow maye knowe howe that proportion will answe the Companies vnder your Chardge, and after yow haue Caused it to be layed vpp in good and suer stowage vnder the Chardge of such ministers as [Bourchier *in margin*] the *Maister of the Ordenance* hathe appointed for the same, yow are to be very warie and circonspect howe the same is to be yssued to the souldiours not impertinentlie as heretofore hathe benne vsed, but with good respect to answer the needfull services, either for trayninge of the Companies, or for theire actuall ymployment abroade against the Ennemies. And for defalcations yow are to see them made accordinge such notes and rates, and with such distinctions as the maister of the Ordenance hathe sett downe and deliuered to his ministers there. Allwayes foreseeing that there be noe powder or other mvnition embeazeled or vnderhand sould whereby it may come to the vse of the Traitour, but sevearely to punishe the offendors whoesoever they be, being Iustlie detected.

And where it is intended as yow knowe to plante another garrison at Ballishannan, Asheroe, or Donegall, over which I the *Lord Deputie* haue appointed Sr. Mathewe Morgan Knight to Commaunde as Cheife whoe hathe his Commissions and instructions accordingelye for that purpose: wee require yow that frequent intelligence maye passe betweene yow and him, and a fast Correspondencie be helde on bothe partes in all matters appertayninge to her majesties service, for the better furtheranee thereof wherein wee require yow to be very Carefull for that the good agreement and faithefull answeringe of one another of yow twoe wilbe a greate stremgthninge to yow both in your severall Chardges, And in that pointe the like direction is gyven to Sr. Mathewe Morgan.

Where it maye fall out and it is very likelie that some of the Irishe bothe of the better, and meaner sorte within the presincte and Juriousdiction of yours maye make meanes to yow to be receaved in bothe vppon pretence to doe service, and vppon Conditiones in which Case it is requisit that before theire takinge in, yow be throwlie enformed of the quallities of the men, and what meanes they haue to doe service, to the ende yow maye knowe, howe farr to truste them, and howe farr to employe them, and for theire better assurance that yow take good pledges of them till yow haue had good prooffe and tryall of theire service. And herein wee wishe yow to hould a discreete and temperat Course to drawe in soe many of the better sorte of Irishe as yow canne, and likewise of the meaner sorte whereby the Arch-traitor maye be weakened, and yow streingthned; In which Course yow are to vse faithefull instruments and yf neede be to sende them amongst the Irishe to Laboure & woorke them, yf of themselves they shall not make offer. Allwaies provided, that in the takinge in of any of them yow drawe in the Condicons, as much as yow can to be honorable for Her Majestie and profittable for Her service.

ffor that vppon those Seaes the Scottishe gallyes and boates are frequent seene by waye of trade with the Subiects of the Northe partes of that Realme and some to houlde entercouse with the Rebbells and to bring them victualls and other necessaries: yow are to gyve order to your Crompstres, barques and barges employed in that service to doe theire best to stopp those Scottish

gallies and boates as haue trade with the Rebbells and breake theire entercouse with them, makinge bootie of them and theire gallies yf yow shall
fynde them traydinge, with the Rebbells or to bringe them any releefe of victualls powder or mvnitions and shall iustlie proue the same but for those that
shall trade with the Subiect yow are to favoure and Countenaunce them as
beinge the subiects of the Kinge of Scotts, whoe is in ametye and leage with
her Majestie. And in all this Course with the Scottishe boates and gallis, yow
are in any wise to foresee yow doe nothinge, nor Cause any thinge to be
doene to the breach of the leage betweene Her majestie and the Kinge of
Scotlande, but to vse all meanes in your proceedinges to entertaine and
Conserve all ametie and good Neighthourehood betweene the twoe Realmes
gyving yow hereby full power and aucthoritye to Comon, parlie, treate and
protect such of that nacon as yow shall thinke good for her majesties service
for such tyme as yow shall thinke meete.

Lastlie where Sr. Mathewe Morgan hathe by his Commission vnder the
Seale, Juriousdiccon over the Countrey of ffermanaughe ortherwise Called
Maguires Countrey and for that there maye be occasion for yow to haue
dealinge in that Countrey in some sorte for the advancement of her majesties
service, either for protectinge, parleying or treatinge with anie of that
Countrey for the benefit of the service, or otherwise vppon further advantage
to be taken to vse prosecution with force, we wishe and doe require yow in
this Case that yow houlde good intelligences of theese poynts with Sr.
Mathewe Morgan, and to signifye vnto him your proceedinges in what
Countrey of ffermannaugh at all tymes for that is a Countrey lymited and
apporconed within his lettres pattents, and yet vppon good occasion of service yow maye haue intermedlinge therein in sorte as is here lymited. Allwaies
fore seeinge that yow avoide as neere as yow Canne all preiudice to the Saide
Sr. Mathewe Morgan in that parte of his goverment, geaven at her Majesties
Castle of Dublin

Marcij 1599.

It is to be remembred that Sr. Mathewe Morgan hath the like instructions for
his goverment of Ballishannan &c. savinge the difference of the names of the
gouernors and theire seuerall goverments, and savinge likewise that there is
noe Clause for an Hospitall in Sr Mathewe Morgans instructions for that
there was noe direction for it out of Englande.

*Bibl. Lambeth, No. 621, Fol. 75.*

Sr Henrie Dockwraye Knight, Cheefe Commander, and gouernor of all Her
majestie's forces of Horse and foote appointed to reside a Loughefoile, and

the parts there abouts.

The Circuit of His Commaund to Containe the whole Countrey of Tyrone, the County of Armaghe to the Blackewater, with all O'Cane's Countrey, and all other Countreyes, betweene the River of the Bann, in Tyrone, and Horne head in Tyrconnell, all O'Doghertyes Countrey. All mc Swyne ffanaught's Countrey, Lougheswilly, and mc Swyne Edoes Sonnes and followers, and all Con O'Donnell's Sonnes, theire Countreyes and followers.

Sr Henry Dockwray to haue Commission vnder the greate Seale with Ample aucthoritie, to governe and Commaund all theese Countreys and all the seuerall scepts and Nationes within every of them.

To Haue Aucthoritie to prosequite with fyer and swoord, all the rebbells what soeuer within this Circuit, and to Common and treate with any Rebbell, yf occasion soe require, either by Himself, or any other whome hee shall ymploye.

And likewise, to parle and protect, for what tyme in his discrescion hee shall thinke good, and to receaue to mercy any Rebbells vpon such Condicones as Hee shall thinke requisit, for her Majestie's advantage.

Sr Henry Dockwray to haue vnder the great Seale Comission for the mar-shall Lawe, with instructiones vsuall for the same.

Sr Henrie Dockwray to haue a standinge fee for this goverment of xiijs. iiijd. Sterlinge per diem.

Sr Henrie Dockewraye to Haue generall instructions, for the manner of his goverment, and particuler direction to errect an Hospitall for sicke and hurte Souldiours, and to Accomodate that with all things requisitt, according such provisions as are sent out of England.

Sr Henry Dockwray vppon any vrgent occasion of service to Call a Counsell at warr, and to take the Assistance of the best Experienced Capptens and officers in the whole Regiment.

The Crompsters, and all other barges and boates assigned for that service to bee ready att all tymes to Answer Sr Henry Dockwraye.

That a good Correspondencie be held, betweene Sr Henrey Dockwraie and Sr Mathewe Morgan, and frequent Intelligence for the better furtherance of the service.

Sr Henrie Dockwraie either by Himself, or anie other whome he shall ymploye, to enter at any tyme, as occasion shall serve for Her majestie's ser-vice, into the Countrey of ffermannogh, Called Maguire's Countrey, either for proseqution or pacification with any Rebbells, and others in that Countrey, and to parle and protect any Rebbell of that Countrey at all tymes as Hee shall haue occasion for Her majesties' service.

Itt is requisitt, and soe wee doe require, that betweene yow and Sr Mathew Morgan, (Commandinge at Bellishannon,) there be noe Contention or strivinge, either for prioritie of place, or for boundes and meeres of your seuerall goverments, But that there bee a faste vnity and agreement betweene yow bothe, as betweene two servitors, ymployed to one end; Namely, to doe Her Majestie the best service yow can, within your seuerall Circuitts.

And otherwayes by your Disagrements and Contentions, (yf any should bee) Her majestie's purpose might not only bee greatelie disapointed and Dishonored, but allso your self much scandalized, as persones that should more prefer your privat emulacones, then the good of the publique service and aboue all things, wee require that there be noe intermedlinge or Intrudinge in one another's gouerment.

Sr Mathew Morgan, Knight, cheefe Commander and gouernor of all her Majestie's forces of Horse and foote appointed for Bellishannon and the partes thereabouts.

The Circuitt of his Commaunde to Containe Bellishanon, Asheroe, Tyrehugh, and all that Countrey betweene Bellishanon, Donnegall, and Barnismore, vnto the vtmost partes of Barnismore esteward: All O'Boyle's Countrey and his followers, and all mc Swyne Bonaught's Countrey and his followers.

Sr Mathewe Morgan to Haue Commission for Gouerment vnder the greate Seale, and all other things for his Circuit as Sr Henrie Dockwraye had.

The Four Masters call Docwra "Henry Docura, an illustrious knight of wisdom and prudence: a pillar of battle and conflict:" For various notices of this remarkable man the reader is referred to Erck's Repertory of the Patent Rolls of Chancery, pp. 11, 20, 48, 106, 115, 126, 128, 156, 165, 183, 212, and the suppressed work "Patent Rolls of James I." pp. 304, 360.

On the 19th of July in the 14th year of James I.'s reign, he was appointed Treasurer at war, during the King's pleasure, fee 6s. 8d, a day; and on the 15th of May, 1621, he was created Baron of Culmore: The Passage relative to his creation as given in the *Liber Hibernioe* from Lodge's Baronetage is as follows:

"Sir Henry Docwra, Knt. (Treasurer of wars) – Title Lord Docwra, Baron of Culmore, Co. Derry – Patent, Westminster, May 15, 1621 – 20 Jac. I. 2d pars. d. Extinct."

Sir Henry was succeeded by his only son Theodore, the second Lord Docwra of Culmore, who must have died during the interregnum and with him the title, as it does not appear in the lists of the nobility after the restoration of Charles II. In the "Catalogue of the nobility of Ireland, as they ought to sit on the first day of the Parliament holden at Dublin, the 16th day of March, 1639," given in the *Liber Hiberniae*, we have "Theodore, Lord Docwra of Culmore."

The race of Sir Henry Docwra is therefore extinct in the male line, but it appears from Archdall's edition of Lodge's Peerage, that Elizabeth, younger daughter of Henry Lord Docwra, Baron of Culmore was the third wife of Sir Henry Brooke of Brookesborough, who died 31st of August, 1671, leaving by her a son George Brooke, Esq. so that his blood may remain in Ireland through that George.

There are many persons of the name Dockrey in the County of Roscommon, but these are of the sept of the Sil-Muireadhaigh, and are really O'Docraidhs or O'Dockreys. See the Stowe Catalogue, Codex iii. fol. 28, and Hardiman's Edition of O'Flaherty's *Chorographical Description of West Connaught,* p. 140.

# NOTES TO THE PRECEDING TRACT

P. 42 — *The army consisting in list of 4000 foote, and 200 horse, &c.* The Four Masters assert that he had six thousand men, and that he landed first in the harbour of Dublin; but the Irish had this account from common report only, and Docwra's own account is unquestionably more correct. See Annals of the Four Masters, Ed. J. O'D. A.D. 1600, p. 2189, note y.

P. 42 — *Knockfergus.* This is the usual name by which, at this period, English writers were wont to call the town of Carraig Fearghusa, or Carrickfergus, in the County of Antrim.

P. 43 — *Culmore* is in Irish called *Cuil mor*, and translated *angulus magnus*, by Philip O'Sullevan Beare. This fort was described as follows, by Sir Josias Bodley, in September, 1608, as appears from a MS. in the British Museum, Lansdowne, No. 156, 80, (327):–

> "The fort of Culmore stands most conveniently to command the entrance of the river of the Derry, and being on a low neck of land, may with 2 or 300 £ charge, be made an Island. It is raised with turfe and earth, which with violence of the weather and beating of the Sea is much decayed. To assure that place against any assaylants, and re-enforce it, as it were fitt, it were requisite to face it with stone to the high water marke at the least, and repaire the parapetts and bulwarkes, also to erect some small buildings for the Captaine, warders and gunners, and to reserve the Castle that there standeth, for a Storehouse for victualls and munition, of which the whole charge may amount to 6 or 700£."

This fort remained unoccupied as a military station, for one hundred and forty-six years, but it was repaired in 1824, by General Hart. [This is incorrect. Culmore was attacked in 1649 and again occupied by Jacobite forces in 1689. W.P. Kelly].

P. 43 — *Ellogh*, in Irish *Aileach* or *Oileach*, i.e. stone-fort. A small fragment of this Castle still remains in a townland of the same name in the parish of Templemore, Co. of Londonderry. This Castle does not occupy the site of the ancient palace of the Kings of Ulster, whose name it bears. The ruins of the palace of Aileach are to be seen on the neighbouring hill of Grianan. See the Ordnance Memoir of the parish of Templemore, *Townlands*, and *Trias Thaum*. P. 181, note 169.

P. 43 — *The Derry*, in Irish *Doire Chalgaich*, which is translated *Roboretum Calgachi* by Adamnan in his *Vita Columbae*. It is more generally called *Doire Choluim Cille* in the Irish Annals from St. Columbkille, who erected a monastery here about the year 546. It is now called Londonderry. For the Charter granted to the town, erected here by Docwra, See Erck's Inrollments of Chancery, pp. 114, 115. Sir Josias Bodley describes the condition of the works here in September, 1608 as follows:– "The Rampier and bulwarks of the ffort at the Derry are much ruined, the Parapitt cleane fallen away. The most part of it must be newly faced with sodds from the foundation, new gates and bridges to be made, the ditch digged deeper and broader in most places, houses of munition, victualles and other purposes, to be made, where-of the charge cannot be lesse then £1200."

The Four Masters describe the situation of the forts erected by Docwra, as follows:– "After landing they erected on both sides of the harbour three forts, with trenches sunk in the earthen, as they had been ordered in England. One of these forts, i.e. Dun na-long, was erected on O'Neill's part of the Country, in the neighbourhood of Oireacht-Ui-Chiarain; and two in O'Domhnaill's Country, one at Cuil-mor in O'Dochartaigh's Country, in the Cantred of Inis-Eoghain, and the other to the South-west of that at Doire-Choluim-Cille. The English immediately commenced sinking ditches around them-selves and raising a strong mound of earth and a large rampart, so that they were in a state to hold out against them. These were stronger and more secure than Courts of lime and stone in the erection of which much time and great labor might be spent. After this they tore down the Monastery and Cathedral, and destroyed all the ecclesiastical edifices in the town, and erect-ed houses and apartments of them."

P. 45 — *Blackwater*, in Irish *Abhainn-mhor*, a celebrated river of Tyrone; Blackwatertown, and Benburb are on it.

P. 45 — *And finding that we stood upon our defensive onelie*. The Four Masters make the following remarks on the same subject:– "As for O'Domhnaill when he perceived that they were not in the habit of going outside their encampments through fear and dread, he made no account of them, and assembled his forces to proceed into the south of Connacht, to plunder the Countries lying on both sides of Sliabh-Echtghe, and especially Thomond. He had good reason for this indeed, for it was these Earls, namely, the Earl of Clanrickard and the Earl of Thomond, who had requested the Lord Justice and the Council to send over this great army, to keep him in his own territory, away from them, for they deemed it too often that he had gone into their territories. Having adopted this resolution, he left O'Dochartaigh, (O'Doherty,) Chieftain of Inis-Eoghain, i.e. John Og, son of John, son of Felim O'Doherty, to watch the foreigners, that they might not come to plunder his territory. He also left Niall Garbh O'Domhnaill, (O'Donnell,) and some of his army encamped against him on the west side of between them and the cantred of Enda, son of Niall." See Annals of the Four Masters, A.D. 1600, p.2193. Ed. J. O'D.

P. 45 — *And now did Sir Mathew Morgan demand his Regiment of 1000 foote and 50 horse, which at first (as I saide before,) were designed for him for a plantation at Ballyshannon.*

See instructions to Sir Henry Docwra, above given, pp89–95.

P. 46 — *On the 1st of June, Sir Arthur O'Neale, son to old Tirloghe Lenogh, &c. came in unto mee, &c.* The Four Masters notice the "going over of this youth," A.D. 1600. The son of O'Neill, namely, Sir Art, the son of Toirdhealbhach Luineach, (Turlough Lenogh,) son of Niall Conallach, son of Art, son of Conn, went over to assist the English, who were fortified at Dun-na-long, in order to wage war against (the Earl) O'Neill. This Art died among the English. This Sir Arthur died on the 28th of October following. The Queen intended creating him Earl of Tyrone." See Moryson Book i. c. 2, and Four Masters, A.D. 1600, p. 2200.

P. 46 — *O'Dogherties side.* Lough Foyle lies between the territories of O'Kane and O'Doherty.

P. 46 — *Greene Castle*, called by the Irish *Caislen nua*, i.e. New Castle. The ruins of this great Castle, which was erected by the Red Earl of Ulster, in the year 1305, are situate near the western margin of Lough Foyle, in the parish of Moville, barony of Inishowen and Co. of Donegal. See Annals of the Four Masters, A.D. 1305, note h. and also the years 1332 and 1555.

P. 46 — *Sir John Chamberlaine.* Compare Annals of the Four Masters, A.D. 1600, p. 2225, note f.

P. 47 — *Dunalong*, in Irish *Dun-na-long*, i.e. fort of the Ships, now Donalong or Dunnalong, situate on the east-side of the river Foyle in the Barony of Tirkeeran, and County of Londonderry. See Annals of the Four Masters, A.D. 1600, p. 2192. Sir Josias Bodley describes the condition of this fort as follows, in September, 1608: "The greate entrenchment at Dunalonge is more fitt to be raised then repaired, but the peece of ground within the same neare the river which is held by the ward, having no other defence but a deep and broad ditch about it, at this time if it were sufficiently walled on the inside of the ditch, which considering the stone at hand, and the small circuite of the place, will not cost above £150; I should think it of good strength for a ward of 10 or 12 men, and capable of more if need required."

P. 47 — *Moyler Morough mac Swyndoe*. He was called by the Irish *Maelmuire mac Suibne na dTuat* i.e. Maelmuire Mac Suibhne na d-Tuath. He was Chief of Tuatha Toraighe, and had been the chief leader of O'Domhnaill's *Galloglaich* or Gallowglasses.

P. 47 — *He got to the number of 60 into his power*. This is probably a mistake, for 160. P. O'Sullevan Beare makes the number 168. The Four Masters give the following account of this transaction:–

> "As for O'Domhnaill, he remained with his troops, without making any excursion (out of Tirconnell) from the time that he returned from the aforesaid expedition in Thomond to the September following. After his soldiers and hirelings had, within this period, rested themselves, he summoned them to him, to see whether he could get any advantage of the English. He was informed that the horses of the English were sent out every day under the charge of a party of English Cavalry to graze upon a grassy field that was opposite the town, i.e Derry: when he heard of this, he began to meditate how he could make a descent upon those horses; and this is what he did: he took privately, in the darkness of the night, a large party of his soldiers, and a squadron of cavalry, (amounting to no less than six-hundred between horse and foot,) to the brink of a steep rocky valley, which is on the flat mountain to the north of Derry, from whence they could plainly see the people of the town, who could not easily see them. He placed a small party of his cavalary in ambush for the horses and the keepers, at concealed places not far from the town, so as to prevent them from returning to the town when they should wish to do so. They remained thus in ambush until the break of day when they perceived the horses with their keepers coming across the bridge as usual. O'Domhnaill's cavalry set out after them, and attacked and slew some of the keepers; but others made their escape by means of the fleetness and swiftness of their horses. O'Domhnaill's people then commenced driving off as many of the English horses as had been left behind in their power. The main body of their own force coming up to assist them against the English, they sent the horses before them. O'Domhnaill ordered a party of his calvalry to go off with the horses to a secure place. This was accordingly done; and O'Domhnaill remained behind with a body of his cavalry which he selected, and with his foot soldiers."

"When the English perceived that their horses had been taken away from them, they immediately arose, and taking their arms, set out in pursuit of O'Domhnaill. The General, Sir Henry Docwra, with his horsemen mounted on their horses, (i.e. such of them as retained their horses in secure places, and had not lost them on that occasion,) joined in the pursuit as rapidly as they were able. When O'Domhnaill saw the cavalry of the English in full speed after him, he remained behind his infantry, with his troop of cavalry, until the English came up with him. They made a courageous attack upon O'Domhnaill for the recovery of their spoils, and of what was under their protection. O'Domhnaill sustained the onset valiantly and resolutely, and a fierce battle was fought between both parties. One of O'Domhnaill's kinsmen, namely, Aedh, the son of Aedh Dubh, son of Aedh Ruadh, made a well-aimed cast of a javelin at the General, Sir Henry Docwra, and striking him directly in the forehead, wounded him very severely. When the General was thus pierced, he returned back; and the English, seeing their chief, their adviser, and their mighty man, wounded, returned home in sorrow and disgrace, and pursued their horses no further. O'Domhnaill's people proceeded to their tents, and on reckoning the horses which they had carried off, they found them to exceed two hundred in number. O'Domhnaill afterwards divided the horses among his gentlemen, according to their deserts."

P. 48 — *I was stricken with a horseman's staffe in the forehead.* According to the Life of Aedh Ruadh or Red Hugh O'Donnell, by Peregrine O'Clery, Docwra was struck on this occasion with a javelin by Aedh, son of Aedh Dubh O'Domhnaill, the Achilles of the Gaeidhil, or Irish race. P. O'Sullevan Beare says that Docwra was pierced through the helmit by Hugo Junior O'Donellus: "Secundo die quam in terram exsiluerunt Odonellus occurrens centum sexaginta octo equos eith adimit, et rursus equos juxta oppidum pascentes Catholici rapiunt, quas sequuntur Angli. Equestre proelium. Hugo Odonellus cognomento Junior Docrium telo per galeam fixo fracto cranio vulnerat." *Hist. Cathol. Iber.* tom. 3, lib. 6, c. v. fol. 171. See also Annals of the Four Masters, Ed. J. O'D. A.D. 1600, p. 2208.

P. 48 — *Roory brother to O'Cane.* The Four Masters have left us no account of the doings of this person.

P. 51 — *On the third day of October came in Neale Garvie O'Donell.* The Four Masters give the following account of the treacherous proceedings of Niall Garbh O'Domhnaill:[1]

"O'Domhnaill remained besieging the English, without moving from his territory, until the end of October, when he began to make preparations to go again into Thomond, to plunder it. After having come to this resolution, he assembled his forces, and made no delay until he came westwards across the Sligeach, and to Baile-an-mhotaigh. He left Niall Garbh; the son of Conn, son of Calbhach, son of Maghnus O'Domhnaill, behind him in the territory, to defend it against the English, and prevent them from plundering it.

"The English (now) began privately to entreat and implore Niall Garbh O'Domhnaill (to join them), offering to confer the chieftain-ship of the territory upon him, should they prove victorious. They promised him, moreover, many rewards and much wealth, if he would come over to their alliance. He listened for a long time to their offers; and his misfortune at length permitted him to go over to them,[2] by the evil counsel of envious and proud people who were along with him; but for this he was afterwards sorry. His three broth-ers, namely, Aedh Buidhe, Domhnall, and Conn, joined him in this revolt. The English were, no doubt, the better of their going over to them: for they were weary and fatigued for want of[3] sleep and rest every night, through fear of O'Domhnaill; and they were diseased and distempered in consequence of the narrowness of their situation,[4] and the old victuals, the salt and bitter flesh-meat they used, and from the want of fresh meat, and other necessaries to which they had been accustomed. Niall O'Domhnaill provided them with everything they stood in need of, and relieved them from the narrow prison in which they were confined.

"He took ten hundred warriors with him to Leith-bhear (Lifford,) a town upon the banks of the same loch,[5] and a celebrated residence of O'Domhnaill: but at this time the place was not fortified: for there had not been any strong fortress or castle of lime and stone there for a long time before (the one there last having been destroyed) or any thing but a small rampart of earth and sods, surrounded by a narrow, shallow ditch of water, as preparations for the erection of a fortress similar to the one which had been there before.

"The guards, as soon as they perceived the English approaching, vacated this fort through dread and fear, because O'Domhnaill was not near (to assist) them. The English thereupon entered the fort and raised large mounds and ramparts of earth and stone to shelter them; so that they were sufficiently fortified to hold out against their ene-mies.

"One of O'Domhnaill's faithful people followed after him with infor-mation concerning the state of the country, and told him what had happened in his absence. O'Domhnaill was much surprised and amazed that his kinsman and brother-in-law had thus turned against him, for Nuala, the sister of O'Domhnaill, was the wife of Niall. O'Domhnaill returned from the province of Connacht; for he had not passed westwards beyond Baile-an-Mhotagh when the news overtook him, and his forces as quickly as they were able; but (no part of) his soldiers were able to keep pace with him, except a few of his cavalry, and he arrived in the neighbourhood of Leith-bhear aforesaid. The English had not been able to make preys or depredations before O'Domhnaill returned back, but were (employed) strengthening their fortress, and erecting ramparts; and when they heard that O'Domhnaill had arrived, they were afraid[6] to come out of their fort for any thing they wanted.

"O'Domhnaill remained at a place not far from the English, until some of his foot-soldiers had come up with him. O'Domhnaill thought it too long the English remained without being attacked, and he did not wait for the coming up of (the main body of) his army, but exhibited before the English the small number he had, on the south side of Cruachan-Lighean,[7] to the north of the river. When the English perceived him they marched out to meet him, with Niall Garbh O'Domhnaill and his brothers in the van, as leaders of the battle."

"They skirmished with each other, but there was not obstinate conflict on that first day, though they continued in readiness for each other; for the English thought that O'Domhnaill was in want of forces,[8] as he (really) was; and fearing that an ambush might be laid for them, so that they did not wish to go far from the town for that reason. It was the same case with O'Domhnaill's people. It would be unwise in them to come in collision with the enemy so near their fort, with the small force of which they consisted. They (at length) separated from each other, though not in peace or friendship. Some were wounded on both sides by the discharging of javelins, arrows, and leaden balls; but more of[9] O'Domhnaill's people were wounded in this skirmish on account of the fewness of their number.

"The English then proceeded to their houses, and O'Domhnaill and his people went to their tents; and it was with anger and indignation that O'Domhnaill returned thither; for it grieved him that his army had not come up with him on that day; for he was certain that, if he had had them with him at that time, the English would not have escaped from his as they did. O'Domhnaill afterwards, when his army had come up with him, laid a close seige to the English, and pitched his camp within two thousand paces of Leith-bhear above-mentioned, in order to protect his husbandmen, so that they might save the corn crops in the neighbourhood of the English. He sent out spies and scouts every night to reconnoitre the town, and not to permit any one to pass in or out, unless they should pass southwards across the river; and he left no road or passage within one thousand paces of the town upon which he did not post guards and ambuscades, to watch and spy the English, and hinder them from passing out unnoticed, but especially the sons of Conn O'Domhnaill and their people, for these he considered were difficult to be watched, and it was on account of them that his sentinels and ambuscades were so numerous.

"He remained here for the period of thirty days, during which time the people of the country were enabled to save their corn and carry it away in small baskets and sacks, on steeds and horses, into the fastnesses of the country beyond the reach[10] of their enemies.

"On one occasion O'Domhnaill, before he left this camp, went towards the English, to see if he could induce them to come outside the fortifications on the level plain. When O'Domhnaill's people had arrived opposite the town, the English began to reconnoitre them; but they did not sally out against them, for they perceived it was to offer defiance and challenge for battle they had come.

"O'Domhnaill's people then returned back when they did not obtain what they wanted, and they halted for some time on the brink of a river called Dael,[11] a short distance to the north of the town. Large parties of them went to their tents, and about other business, for they did not think that the English would follow them on that day. When Niall Garbh O'Domhnaill perceived O'Domhnaill's people scattered and unprepared for action, he told the English that they ought now to attack them. The English at his bidding armed themselves quietly and silently in the centre of their fortifications, in order that their enemies could not see them until they were armed and accoutred. When they were ready they sallied out from their fortifications in battle array, and then, with Niall and his brothers and people in the van, advanced against O'Domhnaill's people.

"O'Domhnaill saw them advancing, and rejoiced at seeing them coming; and he placed his soldiers in their proper stations fronting them, with their warlike weapons; and he did not permit to shoot at them until they had arrived at the opposite bank of the river. They afterwards met together hand to hand, and a sharp and furious battle was fought between both parties. The two hosts of cavalry rushed to the charge, and began to fight with large spears and green-headed lances. Niall O'Domhnaill gave Maghnus, brother of O'Domhnaill, a thrust of a sharp, long lance under the shoulder-blade, and, piercing the armour with which he was clad, he buried it in his body, and wounded his internal parts. When Rudhraighe O'Domhnaill, Righdamhna of Kineal-Conaill, perceived his brother wounded, he made a brave attack upon Niall, and aimed a forcible and furious thrust of a large javelin at Niall's breast; but Niall raised up the front of the high-rearing foreign steed which he rode, so that the spear struck the steed in the forehead, and penetrated to his brain. Rudhraighe broke the socket of the javelin in drawing it back by the thong, and left the iron blade buried in the horse; so that he held but the handle of it in his hand. The steed[12] finally died of this.

"Wo is me that these heroes of Kineal-Conaill were not united in fight on one side against their enemies, and that they were not at peace, for, while they remained so, they were not banished or driven from their native territories, as they afterwards were!

"As for the English, while the cavalry were battling with each other, they faced O'Domhnaill's infantry in a body, and drove them a short distance before them; but, however, only a few of them were wounded; for the English did not pursue them from the field of contest, because their leader[13] had been wounded in the conflict; and they were obliged to return with thim to Leith-bhear, where he aferwards died. A great number of O'Domhnaill's people pursued them for a long distance, and continued to shoot at and cut them down with the sword, so that numbers of them were slain and wounded. The pursuers thought that they should have defeated them (the enemy) if the main host pursued them further; but fear did not permit those who had been repulsed in the beginning to pursue them again.

"When the English went away O'Domhnaill returned to his tents. And dispirited and melancholy were they that night in the camp, on account of the son of their chief,[14] and their Righdamhna (if he should survive his brothers), being in a dying state.

"As soon as O'Domhnaill arrived at the camp he ordered a litter of fair wattles to be made for Maghnus O'Domhnaill, (on which) to carry him over Bearnus. This was done according to orders. Many of his dear friends and faithful people accompanied him to Dun-na-gall, where a sick man's couch was prepared for him, and O'Domhnaill's physicians were brought to cure him; but they could effect no cure for him. They gave him up for death. There was a Monastery in the neighbourhood of the fortress in which were sons of life,[15] of the order of St. Francis; and the wisest of these were wont to visit him, to hear his confession, to preach to him, and to confirm his friendship with the Lord. He made his confession without concealment, wept for his sins against God, repented his evil thoughts and pride during life, and forgave him who had wounded him, declaring that he himself was the cause, as he had made the first attack. Thus he remained for a week, prepared for death every day, and a select father of the aforesaid order constantly attending him, to fortify him against the snares of the devil. He received then the body of the Lord, and afterwards died on the 22nd of October, having gained the victory over the devil and the world. He was interred in the burial-place of his ancestors in the aforenamed monastery.

"His father, i.e. Aedh, the son of Maghnus, son of Aedh Dubh, was at this time a very old man, living in a state of dotage near the monastery. He was informed of the death of his son; he was greatly affected; and he was in a decline for some time afterwards. His confessors[16] were always instructing him respecting the welfare of his soul.

"This Aedh, the son of Maghnus, son of Aedh Og, son of Aedh Ruadh, son of Niall Garbh, died on the 7th of December. He had been Lord of Keneal-Conaill, Inis Eoghain, and Lower Connacht, for twenty-six years, until he was weakened by the English, and bestowed his lordship, with his blessing, on his son, Aedh Ruadh after he had escaped from the English. This Aedh, the son of Maghnus had attained the lordship after the death of his brother Calbhach, without treachery or fratricide, war or disturbance.

"He was a valiant and warlike man and victorious in his fights and battles before and during his chieftainship and the preyer and plunderer of the territories far and near that were bound to obey him, asserting the right of his tribe from them until he made them obedient to him; a man who had laid aside the cares and anxieties of the world after having given up his lordship to his son, and who was a good earner in the sight of God, meriting rewards for his soul for a period of eight years until he died at this period. He was interred with due honor and veneration in the monastery of St. Francis at Dun-na-gall, in the burial-place of the lords who had successively preceded him.

"As for O'Domhnaill, at the expiration of the thirty days during which he continued besieging the English, he prepared to leave the place in which he had been during that period, and to go to another place not less secure, a little further from the English, on the west brink of the River Finn, between them and Bearnas; for he was afraid (of the effects) of the cold, rough, wintry season on his soldiers, who were watching and guarding every night against the English for it was then Allhallowtide; and he thought it time to bring his army to a place of rest after their great labor, for they had not slept at ease for a long time. The forces proceeded to the aforesaid place. They pitched a camp under the shelter of the wood that was in the vicinity of the river. They erected military tents and habitations, and proceeded to cut down the trees around them, and raised a strong rampart between themselves and their enemies, so that it was difficult to get across it to attack them. Here he passed the time until news reached him that two ships had arrived from Spain to the Irish, who were engaged in the war, with money and arms, powder and lead. These ships put in at the harbour of Inbhirmor[17] in Connacht. He sent the same news to O'Neill and went himself to Connacht in the month of December; leaving after him his brother, Rudhraighe O'Domhnaill, with the greater part of his forces, in the camp which we have mentioned, to defend the country. On his arrival in Tir-Fhiachrach of the Muaidhe, he sent messengers to the above-mentioned ships, to request them come into the harbour of Kealla-beaga.[18] He remained himself at Dun-Neill;[19] for it was the festival of the Nativity of the Lord, and he solemnized the first days of the festival with due veneration.

"News came to him that O'Neill had come after him into the country; and he delayed no longer, but set out to meet O'Neill. They met soon after on the road, face to face, and went forthwith to Dun-na-n-gall. Thither the chiefs of the North went to meet them.

The ships aforementioned put in at the harbour of Teilinn,[20] near Kealla-beaga. All the money and other necessaries that were in them (which were sent to the Irish chiefs) were brought to them to Dun-na-n-gall, and divided into two parts, of which O'Neill and his confederates in the war received one, and O'Domhnaill and his allies the other."

P. 51 — *The Ile of Inche.* This is the only island in Loch Swilly, County of Donegal, and lies about one mile off Church-town. It comprises 3,039 English acres which are chiefly under pasture and tillage.

P. 51 — *The Liffer,* in Irish *Lethbhear,* now Lifford, a small assize town on the west side of the River Foyle in the barony of Raphoe and County of Donegal.

P. 51 — *Castle Fyn,* In Irish *Caislean na Finne,* i.e Castle of the (river) Finn, now Castlefinn, a small village on the river from which it derives its name, in the barony of Raphoe and County of Donegal. See Annals of the Four Masters at the years 1434, 1442, 1480, 1531, 1588.

P. 52 — *His own sonne Tirlogh.* This is probablly the Tirlagh O'Neale mentioned in *Pynnar's Survey of Ulster*, as having received a grant of 4000 acres of land in the precint of Dungannon: "Tirlagh *O'Neale* hath four thousand acres. Upon this he hath made a piece of a Bawne, which is five feet high, and hath been so a long time. He hath made no Estates to his tenants, and all of them do plough after the *Irish* manner." — *Harris Hibernica*, p. 211.

The Editor has discovered nothing more of the history of this Tirlogh, or his descendants if he left any.

P. 52 — *Calebeg*, in Irish *Cealla beaga*, i.e. the small churches, now Killybegs, a small town in the barony of Banagh, County of Donegal. According to the Irish accounts these two ships had first put in at Inbhir-mor, now Broad Haven in the Erris, Co. of Mayo, but that they afterwards sailed northwards and put in at Teilinnn harbour, about seven miles westwards of Killybegs. Here the Irish accounts are certainly more correct, as Docwra had the account of the movement of those foreign ships from report only.

P. 52 — *Which I stand not upon to make particular mention of.* The preys and excursions made by Niall Garbh O'Domhnaill and his followers are noticed by the Four Masters as follows:–

> "A.D. 1600. Niall Garbh O'Domhnaill remained with his brothers and with his English at Leith-bhear, as we have already stated, and they made a hosting into Oireacht-Ui-Chathain in quest of prey and booty; and they did not halt until they arrived at the Dianait, (now Burn Dennet, in the Parish of Donaghedy, barony of Strabane, and Co. of Tyrone,) where a great number of O'Neill's people met them. A battle was fought, in which many were slain on both sides, and O'Neill's people were defeated. Niall with his English then returned to their houses in Leith-bhear with many spoils and in triumph.

> "On another occasion after this, Niall with his brothers and with his English went into Tir-Eoghain, (Tyrone,) and the entire of Gleann-Aichle (Glenelly, bar, Strabane,) was plundered by them.

> "They gave another defeat to the sons of Feardorcha son of John, son of Domhnall at Cnoc Buidhbh, (Knockavoe near Strabane,) where they slew many persons. Toirr-dhealbhach Og O'Coinne and several others were taken prisoners, and they afterwards exacted sixty marks for his ransom.

"Baile-Nua (now Newtown Stewart) in Tir Eoghain and Caislean-na-Deirge (Castlederg) were taken by Niall and the English, but they were recovered from them shortly afterwards," p. 2227.

P. 52 — *Phelim Reogh.* He was the head of a sept of the O'Dohertys', called Mac Devitts. For a curious anecdote of this person, see Annals of the Four Masters, A.D. 1595, p. 1979. He afterwards burned the town erected by Docwra at Derry, for which reason the sept of the Mac Devitts are still locally called "Burnderrys".

P. 53 — *About Christmas this yeare died Sir Robert O'Doghertie.* According to the Four Masters he died on the 27th of January, A.D. 1601, and they add, that O'Domhnaill nominated Felim Og, the brother of the deceased, the O'Dochartaigh (O'Doherty); but that the Clann-Ailin, and the Clann-Daibheitt took Cathaeir, the son of the deceased John to Derry, where Sir Henry Docwra styled him O'Dochartaigh to spite O'Domhnaill. Compare also O'Sullevan Beare's *Hist. Cathol. Iber.* fol. 172. It should be remarked that the English did not begin the year with the month of January, their 1601, not commencing till the 25th of March.

P. 55 — *Mac Swyne Fanaght,* i.e Mac Suibhne or Sweeny of Fanad, a territory in the north of Tirconnell, or county of Donegal extending from Lough Swilly to Mulroy Lough, and from the Sea southwards to Rathmelton. See Annals of the Four Masters, A.D. 1186, p. 71, note s. It is divided from O'Doherty's country by a bay of the Sea, that is Lough Swilly.

P. 55 — *Ramullan,* in Irish, *Rath Maelain,* i.e. Maelan's or Mullan's fort, now Rathmullen, a small town consisting of a single street in the west margin of Lough Swilly, in the barony of Kilmacrenan and Co. of Donegal. The Castle of this place was the principal residence of Mac Sweeny Fanad. See Annals of the Four Masters, A.D. 1516, p. 1335, note n.

P. 55 — *Sleuyghy-Art, Slicht Airt,* i.e. the race of Art. The inhabitants of this tract were the descendants of Art, son of Conn Mor, son of Henry O'Neill. The senior of this sept at this time was young Tirlogh, son of Sir Arthur, son of Tirlogh Lenogh.

P. 56 — *Castle Derg,* in Irish, *Caislean na Derge,* i.e. the Castle of the (river) Derg, now Castlederg, a small village in the barony of Omagh, Co. of Tyrone.

P. 56 — *Coolmackatren,* in Irish, *Cuil-mic-an-Treoim,* i.e the corner or angle of Mac an Treoin. This name is now obsolete though not yet altogether forgotten, but it has received the alias name of Castleforward. It is situate on an arm of Loch Swilly, near the boundary of the baronies of Inishowen and Raphoe, Co. of Donegal. See Annals of the Four Masters, A.D. 1440, and 1529.

P. 56 — *Cargan*, in Irish, *Cairrgin*, i.e. a small rock, now Carrigins, a small village on the river Foyle, about three miles to the south of the city of Londonderry. See Annals of the Four Masters, A.D. 1490, p. 1180, note t.

P. 57 — *Newtowne, a Castle in Tyrone*, in Irish, *baile nua*, i.e. new town, now Newtown Stewart, in the barony of Strabane, Co. of Tyrone. See Annals of the Four Masters, A.D. 1600, p. 227, note k.

Sir Josias Bodley describes this place as follows, in September, 1608: "The Newtowne is a place much ruined; howbeit if it be thought fitt to be held, (whereof I can see no necessity, if the Garrisons at O'Magh be increased to any strength,) it may be made sufficiently defensible by some small repayring of the Castle, and raysing the walls that encloseth it in some parts *scarping* the banke towards the river side and casting a ditch about it, whereof the charge may be £150."

P. 58 — *Tirlogh Magnylson*, in Irish, *Toirrdhealbhach Mac Niallghurain.*

P. 58 — *Ainoch, a Castle of O'Caine's*, in Irish, *Eanach*, i.e. Marsh. This Castle is called the Tower of Enagh, by Ware in his Annals, under the year 1555, and "Arx nobilissima familiae O'Cathanorum" by Colgan, who describes its situation as "tertia tantum milliari versus aquilonem distans ab ipsa Civitate Dorensi." *Trias Thaum.* P. 450, note 51. This Castle is shown on several maps of Ulster, made in the reign of James I. as situate on an island in Lough Enagh East, in the parish of Clondermot, near the City of Londonderry. There are no ruins of it at present. See Annals of the Four Masters, A.D. 1555, note h.

P. 58 — *Ballyshannon, beal-atha-Seanaigh*, i.e mouth of Seanach's ford. This is now a considerable town on the river Erne, in the south of the County of Donegal. It appears from several letters of Queen Elizabeth, that she had meditated for a long time to occupy this position, as well as the Derry, with English troops, as absolutely necessary to do service upon the rebels of Tirconnell; but no effectual force was sent till the appointment of Sir Henry Docwra and Sir Mathew Morgan.

P. 59 — *Cormac ma Baron, Cormac mac an barúin*, he was the brother of Hugh, Earl of Tyrone. He possessed the lands around the fort of Augher, in the barony of Clogher, Co. of Tyrone.

P. 60 — *The Abbaye of Dunnagall*, in Irish, Dun na n-gall, i.e. a fort of the foreigners, now Donegal, in the barony of Tirhugh, Co. of Donegal. This monastery was founded for Franciscan friars in the year 1474, by Aedh Ruadh, son of Niall Garbh O'Domhnaill, chief of Tirconnell, and his wife Finola, daughter of Conchobhar na Srona O'Brian, King of Thomond. The remains of the building are still to be seen in tolerable preservation at a short distance from the town of Donegal. See *Annals of the Four Masters*, Ed. J. O'D. Introductory Remarks, pp. xxviii, xxix.

The Four Masters give the following account of the proceedings of Niall Garbh and the English in Tirconnell, from this period until O'Domhnaill set out for Kinsale:

"As soon as O'Domhnaill heard of the arrival of this numerous army at the place which we have before mentioned, he assembled his forces, and did not halt until be crossed the Coirr-sliabh, and the (River) Buille, into Magh-luirg; and pitched his camp directly opposite them (his enemies). They remained thus for some time face to face, spying and watching each other. Many were the conflicts, man-slaughters, and affrays which took place between them while they remained thus in readiness for each other, until (at length) the English army became wearied, and returned in sorrow to their houses.

"After this, news reached O'Domhnaill, that Niall Garbh, the son of Conn, son of Calbhach, with his (O'Donnell's) English and Irish, had come from the east (of Tirconnell), across Bearnas, and encamped at Dun-na-n-gall, in the east of Tir-Aedha. When O'Domhnaill received the news that the English had arrived at that place he felt grieved for the misfortune of the monastery, and that the English should occupy and inhabit it instead of the Sons of Life and the Culdees, whose rightful property it was till then; and he could not forbear from going to try if he could relieve them. What he did was this; he left the farmers and betaghs of Tirconnell, with their herds and flocks throughout Lower Connacht, with some of his soldiers to protect them against (invaders from) the harbours, kerns, and foreign tribes, (and) he himself proceeded with the greater part of his army, across the (rivers) Sligach, Dubh, Drobhaeis, and Eirne, northwards, and pitched his camp in strong position exactly at Carraig, which is upwards of two thousand paces from Dun-na-n-gall, where Niall Garbh O'Domhnaill and his English were (stationed). As for O'Domhnaill he ordered great numbers of his forces alternately to blockade the monastery by day and night, so as to prevent the English from coming outside its walls to destroy anything in the country. Neither of the armies did by any means pass their time happily or pleasantly, for killing and destroying, conflict and shooting, were carried on by each party against the other. The English were reduced to great straits and distress by the long siege in which they were kept by O'Domhnaill's people; and some of them used to desert to O'Domhnaill's camp in twos and threes, in consequence of the distress and straits in which they were from the want of a proper ration of food. Thus they passed the time until the end of September, when God willed to take revenge and satisfaction of the English for the profanation and abuse which they had offered to the churches and apartments of the psalm-singing ecclesiastics, namely of the monastery of Dun-na-n-gall and the monastery of Machaire-beag, in which the English whom we have mentioned were quartered and encamped, and others of them who were in the castle of Dun-na-n-gall.

"The vengeance which God wreaked upon them was this, however it came to pass, viz; fire fell among the powder which they had in the monastery of Dun-na-n-gall for carrying on the war; so that the boarded apartments, and all the stone and wooden buildings of the entire monastery were burned. As soon as the spies and sentinels, whom O'Domhnaill had posted to spy and watch the English, perceived the brown-red mass of flames, and the dense cloud of vapor and smoke that rose up over the monastery, they began to discharge their leaden bullets and their fiery flashes, in order that O'Domhnaill might (hear them, and I) immediately come to them, to attack the English for they thought it would occasion too long a delay to send him messengers. This signal was not slowly responded to by O'Domhnaill and his army, for they vehemently and rapidly advanced with their utmost speed, in troops and squadrons, to where their people were at the monastery. Bloody and furious was the attack which they made upon the English and their own friends and kinsmen who were there. It was difficult and (almost) impossible for O'Domhnaill's people to withstand the fire of the soldiers who were in the monastery and the castle of Dun-na-n-gall, and in a ship which was in the harbour opposite them; yet, however, O'Domhnaill's people had the better of it, although many of them were cut off. Among the gentlemen who fell here on the side of O'Domhnaill was Tadhg, the son of Cathal Og Mac Diarmad, a distinguished captain of the Sil-Maeilruanaidh. On the other side fell Conn Og, the son of Conn, the brother of Niall Garbh O'Domhnaill, with three hundred others, in that slaughter.

"As soon as Niall Garbh O'Domhnaill perceived the great jeopardy in which his people and the English were, he passed unnoticed westwards, along the margin of the harbour, to Machaire-beag, where a great number of the English were (stationed); and he took them with him to the relief of the other party of English, who were reduced to distress by O'Domhnaill and his people; and the crew of the ship proceeded to fight, and kept up a fire in defence of them, until they had passed inside the central walls of the monastery.

"When O'Domhnaill observed the great strength of the place in which they were and the great force that had come to the relief of the English, he ordered his soldiers to withdraw from the conflict and to return back; for he did not deem it meet that they should be cut off in an unequal contest. This was done at his bidding; and he removed his camp nearer to the monastery, and sent some of his people to Machaire-beag, where the English whom Niall Garbh had brought with him to assist his people were (stationed). The burning of the monastery and this occurrence, happened precisely on Michaelmas-day.

"O'Domhnaill remained thus blockading the English, and reducing them to great straits and exigencies, from the end of September to the end of October, without any deed of note bing achieved between them during that time, until news (at length) reached them that a Spanish fleet had arrived in the south of Ireland, to assist the Irish who were at war."

Compare this and Docwra's text with P. O'Sullevan Beare's *Hist Cathol. Iber.* tom. 3, lib. 6, c. 5, fol. 173. Compare also Mooney's account of the burning of the monastery of Donegal in the Rev. M. Kelly's recent edition of O'Sullevan Beare's work.

P. 60 — *A brother of his owne.* According to the Four Masters this was Conn Og, son of Conn. He is the ancestor of Manus O'Donnell, Esq. of Castlebar and of the O'Donnells of Spain and Austria, whose descent, as well as that of Sir Richard O'Donnell of Newport and of the Rev. Constantine O'Donnell, from Conn, Chief of Tirconnell, will be seen in the following genealogical table:–

Colonel Manus O'Donnell, No. 5, *supra*, the ancestor of the Newport family, is set down in the list of Subscribers to Mac Curtin's *Vindication of the Antiquity of Ireland*, as head of a Branch of the O'Donnells. According to the traditions of Ballycroy, he was the son of Roger O'Donnell by a Margaret Sheil, but his legitimacy was questioned by the O'Donnell's of Larkfield and Greyfield, and other members of the family. It was frequently asserted in articles in the Dublin Evening Post by the late Con O'Donnell of Larkfield. This may be the reason why Charles O'Conor of Belanagare makes Hugh O'Donnell of Larkfield the chief of the Tirconnell line. See Dissertations, First Edition, p. 231.

P. 61 — *Newtowne and Castle-Derg.* The Masters inform us that these Castles were recovered from Niall Garbh and the English shortly after they had taken them; but they do not say by what means they were recovered.

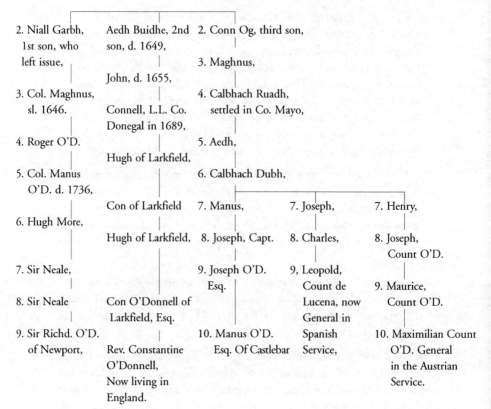

1. Conn, Chief of Tirconnell, d. 1583

2. Niall Garbh, 1st son, who left issue,

Aedh Buidhe, 2nd son, d. 1649,

2. Conn Og, third son,

3. Maghnus,

3. Col. Maghnus, sl. 1646.

John, d. 1655,

4. Calbhach Ruadh, settled in Co. Mayo,

Connell, L.L. Co. Donegal in 1689,

4. Roger O'D.

5. Aedh,

Hugh of Larkfield,

5. Col. Manus O'D. d. 1736,

6. Calbhach Dubh,

Con of Larkfield

7. Manus,

7. Joseph,

7. Henry,

6. Hugh More,

Hugh of Larkfield,

8. Joseph, Capt.

8. Charles,

8. Joseph, Count O'D.

7. Sir Neale,

9. Joseph O'D. Esq.

9, Leopold, Count de Lucena, now General in Spanish Service,

9. Maurice, Count O'D.

8. Sir Neale

Con O'Donnell of Larkfield, Esq.

9. Sir Richd. O'D. of Newport,

Rev. Constantine O'Donnell, Now living in England.

10. Manus O'D. Esq. Of Castlebar

10. Maximilian Count O'D. General in the Austrian Service.

P. 62 — *Ashrowe* in Irish *Eas Ruaidh*, now Assaroe, a townland containing the ruins of an abbey situate about a mile west of Ballyshannon. The name was originally applied to the cataract at Ballyshannon, now called the Salmon Leap.

P. 64 — *Caue Ballagh mac Rickard*, in Irish *Cumhaighe Ballach mac Ricaird*, i.e. Cooey the Freckled, son of Richard.

P. 64 — *Dongevin*, in Irish *Dun Geimhin*, i.e Geimhin's fort, now Dungiven a small town in the barony of Keenaght, Co. of Londonderry. No part of the ruins of this Castle (which stood on the bank of the river Roe to the south of the village) now remain.

P. 64 — *Terwin mac Guirck*, now Termonmagurk in the barony of Omagh, County of Tyrone.

P. 64 — *Omy*, in Irish, *Omaighe*, now Omagh, a town in a barony of the same name County of Tyrone.

P. 64 — *Dongannon*, in Irish *Dun-Geanain*, i.e. Geanain's fort, now Dungannon, a town in a barony of the same name, County of Tyrone. This was the chief residence of Hugh, Earl of Tyrone.

P. 64 — *Lough Sidney*. This was a name given to Loch n-Eathach, or Lough Neagh, in the reign of Queen Elizabeth, from Sir Henry Sidney, Lord Deputy of Ireland.

P. 64 — *Mountjoy*. The ruins of this fort or Castle are situate near Belleville, not far from Stewartstown, in the barony of Dungannon and Co. of Tyrone.

P. 64 — *Charlemont*. The castle of Charlemont is still a place of importance, being the Ordnance depot for the north of Ireland, and head quarters for the artillery of the district. Charlemont and Moy may be said now to form one town, being merely separated by the Blackwater, the former being on the Armagh, and the latter on the Tyrone side of the river.

P. 65 — *Foghan*, now Faughan, a river in the barony of Tirkeeran, Co. of Londonderry, falling into Loch Foyle nearly opposite the fort of Culmore.

P. 65 — *Bangibbon river*. This is unquestionably the river called Dianait by the Irish, and now Burndennet or Bundennet, a stream flowing through the parish of Donaghedy in the barony of Strabane, Co. of Tyrone, and paying its tribute to the river of Loch Foyle, nearly opposite Port Hall in the parish of Clonleigh. *[O'Donovan is in fact mistaken here. There is a stream called the Bangibbagh or Burngibbagh that flows into the River Faughan at Drumahoe. This makes more sense from a territorial point of view.]*

P. 65 — *The Band*, i.e. the river of Lower Bann.

P. 66 — *The honnor of knighthood*. It is not generally known that Sir Cahir O'Doherty was knighted for his bravery in fighting against the O'Neills. Such, however, was the case, as is clear from our author's text. He was as great an enemy to O'Domhnaill as was Niall Garbh, and his rebellion when too late had its origin in a personal insult.

P. 67 — *Clogher*, the head of an ancient bishopric in a barony of the same name and County of Tyrone.

P. 67 — *Augher*, a small town situate two miles to the north-east of Clogher. The castle of this place was situate on an island called Fraechmhagh by the Four Masters at the year 1602, where they have the following passage:

A.D. 1602. "A hosting was made by Niall Garbh O'Domhnaill and the English and Irish along with him, from Fraechmhagh in Tir-Eoghain, by order of the Lord Justice, who was at the same time laying siege to the island of Fraechmhagh. He plundered Cormac, son of the Baron, who was the brother of O'Neill, and also Boston (Harry Hoveden), and the country westwards as far as Machaire Stefanach, and carried many preys and spoils to Fraechmhagh, to the Lord Justice." – p. 2323.

P. 68 — *The Glynns*. Tyrone at this time had betaken himself to the woods of Glenconkeine, near the old church of Ballynascreen in the barony of Loughinsholin, County of Londonderry.

P. 68 — *Sleugh Gillen*, in Irish, *Sliabh Callainn*, i.e Callan's mountain, now *anglice* Slieve Gallion, a remarkable mountain on the confines of the Counties of Londonderry and Tyrone, forming the southern boundary of the great valley of Glenconkeine.

P. 70 — *My Lord wrote for Rorie O'Donnell*. The Four Masters thought that Niall Garbh was offered all Tirconnell to be held by Patent under the Crown of England; but that refusing this he got himself inaugurated O'Donnell at Kilmacrenan, which exasperated the Lord Deputy so much that he set up Rory O'Donnell in preference to him. In this however they were mistaken, for Docwra had so blasted the character of Niall Garbh in the eyes of the Lord Deputy, that he could not be prevailed upon to recommend his being created Earl of Tirconnell. P. O'Sullevan Beare states that Niall Garbh appeared before the Council at Dublin, and asserted that Ireland was conquered not by the arms of England, but by himself, and expressed his great dissatisfaction at the unjust manner in which he was treated by them.

P. 72 — *That hee had now taken in Tyrone*. If Queen Elizabeth had lived a few months longer O'Neill would never have been taken into mercy, for, writing to Mountjoy on the 9th of October, 1602, she says:

> "Lastly, for Tyrone, we do so much mislike to give him any Grace, that hath been the only Author of so much Effusion of blood, and the most ungrateful Viper to us that raised him, and one that hath so often deceived us, both when he hath craved his pardon, and when he hath received it of us, as when we consider how much the World will impute to us of weakness to shew favour to him now, as if without that, we could not give an end to this Rebellion, we still remain determined not to give him Grace of any kind." — *Moryson*, b. III. c. I. vol. II. p. 225.

After this her Majesty's Officers in Ireland had recourse to every stratagem that cunning and subtlety could suggest to take him prisoner or assassinate him; but fortunately for him, he had been educated in their own school, and had learned to avoid them with equal skill and caution. The Lord Deputy complains of *his skill in keeping on his head,* and of the inviolable honor of his followers, who could not be induced by any bribe he could offer, to lay violent hands upon his sacred person, in a letter to the Lords in England written on the 25th of February, 1602–3, from which an extract is here given as a curious specimen of the politics and morals of those times:

> "And it is most sure that never Traitor knew better how to keep his own Head than this, nor any Subjects have a more dreadful Awe to lay violent Hands on their sacred Prince, than these people have to touch the persons of their O'Neals; and he, that hath as pestilent a Judgment as ever any had, to nourish and to spread his own Infection, hath the ancient Swelling and Desire of Liberty in a conquered Nation to work upon, their Fear to be rooted out, & to have their own faults punished upon all particular Discontents, and generally, over all the Kingdome, the Fear of Persecution for Religion, the debasing of the Coin (which is grievous unto all sorts) and a Death and Famine, which is already begun, and must, of Necessity, grow shortly to Extremity, the least of which alone have been many Times sufficient Motives to drive the best and most quiet Estates into sudden confusion. These will keep all spirits from settling, breed new Combinations, and, I fear, even stir the Towns themselves to solicit foreign Aid," &c. &c.

It appears by another letter given by Moryson book iii. c. 2 and dated 25th March 1603, addressed by Mountjoy to Master Secretary, that the designs against O'Neill at the time of his being received unto mercy were exceedingly dark and inhuman.

> "I have received by Captain Hays her Majesty's Letters of the 6th of February, wherein I am directed to send for Tyrone, with promise of security for his life only, and upon his arrival, without further Assurance, to make staye with him till her Pleasure should be further known; and at the same Time, I received another from her Majesty, of the 17th February, wherein it pleased her to enlarge the Authority given unto me, to assure him of Life, Liberty, and Pardon, upon some conditions remembered therein; and withal I received a letter from yourself of the 18th of February, recommending to me your own Advice, to fulfil (as far as I possibly could) the Meaning of her Majesty's first letter, and signifying her Pleasure that I should seek by all the best Means I can, to promise him his Pardon *by some other Name than Earl of Tyrone,* and rather by the name of Baron of Dungannon, or if needs must be, *by the name of some other Earl.* Secondly to deliver him his Country in less Quantity, and with less

Power than before he had. And lastly to force him to clear his Paces and Passages, made difficult by him against any Entry into his Country. And now, since it hath pleased her Majesty, by so great a Trust, to give me so comfortable Arguments of her Favour, I am incouraged the more freely to presume to declare myself in this great Matter, which I call great, because the Consequence is great and dangerous to be dealt in without the Warrant of her gracious Interpretation. And though my opinion herein should proceed from a long and advised Consideration, described with large and many Circumstances, and confirmed with strong and judicial Reasons, yet, because I think it fit to hasten away this Messenger, I will write of these Things somewhat, though on the sudden, and commit the rest to the sufficient judgment and Relation of the Lord President, now in his Journey towards you; and the rather, because I find him to concur with me in the Apprehension of this Cause, and of the State of all other things of this Kingdom. And first for her Majesty's first Letter, I pray you, Sir, believe Me that I have omitted nothing, both by Power and Policy, to ruin him, and utterly to cut him off; and if, by either, I procure his Head, before I have engaged her Royal Word for his Safety, *I do protest I will do it*; and much more be ready to possess myself of his Person, if, by only Promise of Life, or by any other Means whereby I shall not directly scandal the Majesty of publick Faith, I can procure him to put himself into my Power. But to speak my opinion freely, I think that he, or any Man in his Life, which he knoweth how so well to secure by many other Ways; for, if he fly into Spain, that is the least whereof he can be assured and Most men (but especially he) do make little Difference between the value of their Life and Liberty; and to deceive him I think it will be hard, for though Wiser Men than he may be over-reached, yet he hath so many Eyes of Jealousy awake." — Moryson book iii. c. 2, Ed. of 1735, vol. ii. p. 275.

In the mean time Queen Elizabeth died, (on the 24th of March, 1603) and Fynes Moryson boasts that he himself contrived by *laudable* cunning that O'Neill should make his submission to her, though he (Moryson) *knew that she was dead*. He made his submission on his knees at Mellifont on the 30th of March following, but when he heard the news of the Queen's death, he could not refrain from tears, being now a sexaginarian, and seeing the helpless state to which he was reduced by the artifice of his enemies; for the pardon and protection he received rested on the dead body of Elizabeth. He had also lost the opportunity, either of continuing the war against a weak prince, or making a meritorious submission to the new sovereign who was believed to have deduced his descent from the ancient Irish.

The Lord Deputy's honor was however pledged, and accordingly on the 6th of April, he did not only renew his protection in King James's name, but soon after gave him liberty to return to Ulster to settle his affairs; but first, O'Neill, now once more Earl of Tyrone, delivered up hostages, and also renewed his submission in a set form of words, wherein he "abjured all foreign power and jurisdiction in general, and the King of Spain's in particular," and renounced the name of O'Neill and all power and authority over the Urrighs of Ulster and all his lands, except such as should be granted to him by the King; and he promised future obedience, and to discover his correspondence with the Spaniards. At the same time he wrote a letter to the King of Spain, request-ing to send home to him his eldest son Henry, who, however, never returned, for he was soon after strangled at Brussels. See the Rev. M. Kelly's Edition of O'Sullevan's Beare *Hist. Cathol. Iber.*

P. 72 — *It was Treason by the Law.* Mountjoy was certainly mistaken in this.

P. 74 — *And as another writing a Discourse upon the Battaile of Kinsaile.* This evidently alludes to Fynes Moryson's account of the victory at Kinsale.

P. 81 — *Brake out into open Rebellion, but that fell out a good while after.* O'Doherty broke out into open rebellion, in 1608, and was slain under the rock of Doon near Kilmacrenan, on the 5th of July that year, as appears by an Inquisition taken 6th Jac. I. See Annals of the Four Masters, A.D. 1608, p. 2358, and P. O'Sullevan Beare's *Hist. Cathol. Iber.* Tom. 4, lib 1, cap. V.

The Four Masters give the following account of the proceeding of the O'Domhnaill, from the period of the defeat at Kinsale to that of the death of Aedh, Earl of Tyrone, at Rome. See Annals of the Four Masters, p. 2324, 5.

> "As for O'Neill and the Irish (adherents) who remained in Ireland after the defeat at Kinsale, what O'Domhnaill (Aedh Ruadh) had instructed and commanded them to do, before his departure for Spain, was to exert their bravery in defence of their patrimony against the English; until he should return with forces to their relief, and to remain in the camp in which they (then) were, because their loss was small, although they had been routed. He had observed to them also that it would not be easy for them to return safe to their country, if that were their wish, because their enemies and adversaries would pursue and attack them; and those who had been affectionate and kind towards them, on their coming into Munster, would be spiteful and malicious towards them on their return to their territories, and that they would attack and plunder them, and scoff at and mock them.

"The chiefs of the Irish did not, however, take his advice, and did not attend to his request, because he himself was not among them; but they resolved on returning to their territories. They afterwards set out in separate hosts, without ceding the leadership to any one lord; but each lord and chieftain apart, with his own friends and faithful people following him. Alas! how different were the spirit, courage, energy, hauteur, threatening, and defiance of the Irish, on their return back at this time, from those they had when they first set out on this expedition. The surmises of the Prince O'Domhnaill, and every thing which he predicted, were verified; for, not only did their constant enemies rise up before and after them to give them battle, but their (former) friends, confederates and allies, rose up, and were attacking and shooting them on every narrow road through which they passed. It was not easy for the chiefs and gentlemen, the soldiers and warriors, to protect and defend their people, on account of the length of the way that lay before them, the number of their enemies, and the severity and inclemency of the boisterous winter season, for it was then the end of winter precisely. Howbeit they reached their territories after great dangers, without any remarkable loss; and each lord of a territory began to defend this patrimony as well as he was able.

"Rudhraighe O'Domhnaill, the son of Aedh, son of Maghnus, was he to whom O'Domhnaill had, on the night before his departure, left the government of his people and lands, and everything which was hereditary to him, until he should return back again; and he had commanded O'Neill and Rudhraighe to be friendly to each other, as themselves both had been. They promised him this thing.

"The Kineal-Conaill then thronged around the representatve of their prince, though most of them deemed the separation from their former hero and leader as the separation of soul from body. O'Domhnaill's son, Rudhraighe, proceeded to lead his people with resoluteness and constant bravery through every difficult and intricate passage, and through every danger and peril which they had to encounter since they left Kinsale until they arrived, in the very beginning of spring, in Lower Connacht, where the cows, farmers, property, and cattle of the Kineal-Conaill were (dispersed) throughout the country, in Corann, in Luighne, and in Tir-Fhiachrach of the Muaidhe. God was the herdsman and shepherd who had come to them thither; for although O'Domhnaill, at his departure, had left his people much of the cattle of the neighbouring territories, Rudhraighe did not suffer them to be forcibly recovered from him by any territory from which they had been taken; for he distributed and stationed his soldiers and warriors upon the gaps of danger and the undefended passes of the country, so that none would attempt to come through them to plunder or persecute any of his people.

"O'Gallchubhair (Eoghan the son of John), had been keeping the castle of Baile-an-mhotaigh for O'Domhnaill, since he set out for Munster, until this time; but as soon as Rudhraighe returned he gave the castle up to him, so that it was under his command."

"The castle of Baile-atha-Seanaigh, in which guards had been placed by O'Domhnaill, was taken by Niall Garbh O'Domhnaill and the English, after they had broken and greatly battered it by a great gun which they had carried to it; and the warders, seeing that there was no assistance or relief at hand, escaped from it by flight. This castle was taken in spring.

"Inis-Saimer (at Ballyshannon) and Inis-mic-Conaill were taken by Aedh Buidhe, the son of Conn O'Domhnaill; and Cormac the son of Donnchadh Og Meg-Uidhir, was also taken prisoner by him.

"Niall Garbh, with his brothers, and the English, went in boats on Loch Eirne, and took and destroyed Inish-keithlinn. They also took (the monasteries of) Daimhinis and Lisgabhail, and left warders in them.

"Mac Suibhne Bagh-aineach (Donnchadh the son of Maeil-muire) came over to Niall O'Domhnaill and the English. Niall and Mac Suibhne fought a battle with a party of the Meg-Uidhir and Mac Cabas, in which many were slain; and Brian, the son of Dubh-gall Mac Caba, was taken prisoner by them.

"The island of Cill-Tighearnaigh, (Killierny bar. of Lurg) in Fermanagh, was taken by Domhnall, the son of Conn O'Domhnaill; and he carried off many spoils from it.

"Aedh Buidhe, the son of Conn O'Domhnaill, took a prey from Tuathal, son of Felim Dubh O'Neill, in the country of the Slicht-Airt O'Neill.

"Sir Oliver Lambert came in the summer to Sligeach with a numerous army of English and Irish, and there encamped against Rudhraighe O'Domhnaill, who was to the south of them, and against (the inhabitants of) Lower Connacht in general to try whether they could seize on any of their property. Cath-bhar, the son of Aedh Dubh O'Domhnaill, went and ratified his peace and friendship with Sir Oliver. The place at which Cath-bhar had his residence and fortress at this time was Dun-Aille, (Dunally) to the west of Sligeach; (and) Sir Oliver and Cathbhar prepared to go with their forces into Fermanagh, in search of prey and spoils.

"As soon as Rudhraighe O'Domhnaill hear of this expedition, it grieved him that his allies and friends should be plundered, without coming to their relief, if he could; and he repaired to O'Ruaire (Brian Og), to request of him to join his forces, that they might engage the English at a pass where he expected to get an advantage of them. He also requested him to assist him in the war until O'Domhnaill should return to relieve the Irish, and to give him one of his strong impregnable castles, as a resting place for his wounded, disabled, feeble, and sick people; and, moreover, that he would allow his people (to remove) with their property and cattle into his territory. O'Ruaire refused the son of O'Domhnaill everything he requested of him, and the other was grieved and insulted at his refusal; but seeing that he was not strong enough to cope with the English, he remained to protect his own people.

"As for Sir Oliver, he and Cath-bhar went, with their muster, and plundered the neighbouring parts of Fermanagh; and, after carrying off many spoils, they returned to their houses.

"Sir Oliver was informed of the proceedings of Rudhraighe O'Domhnaill, and how he had requested of O'Ruaire to join him, to obstruct him (Sir Oliver) in the expedition which we have before mentioned, and his animosity against him grew greater on account of it; and he, therefore, sent for additional forces to Athluain, to wreak his vengeance upon Rudhraighe. As soon as Rudhraighe heard that the English of Athluain were approaching him from the south side, and the English of Sligeach from the other side, he collected his property, his cattle, flocks, and herds, (and moved) with them across Coirrshliabh-na-Seaghsa into Magh-luirg, from thence across the Sinann into Muintir-Eolais, and to Sliabh-an-Iarainn, in Conmaicne-Rein; so that the English seized no portion of them; and the English of Athluain returned to their homes without gaining any victory on that occasion. The people of the son of O'Domhnaill (then) returned back again with their cattle to the places from which they had set out, namely to Corann, Luighne, and Tir-Fhiachrach.

"Rudhraighe himself then set out with all his forces, and arrived at the island of Loch-Iasgach (Esk) to the east side of Dun-na-n-gall, where O'Domhnaill's warders were, and where O'Conchobhair Sligeach was left in custody, since he had been taken by O'Domhnaill until the end of that summer. When he came to this castle, his people there were much rejoiced at his arrival. O'Conchobhair promised to be entirely submissive to O'Domhnaill's son; and after they had entered into a treaty of friendship with each other, he released O'Conchobhair from captivity; and they afterwards returned back to Connacht.

"At this time, that is, in autumn, the English of Rosscomain and Upper Connacht mustered a numerous army, to march against Rudhraighe O'Domhnaill again; and they did not delay until they arrived at the monastery of Buille. Rudhraighe and O'Conchobhair mustered another army to meet them; and they marched across Coirrshliabh, and pitched their camp before the town at the other side. They took their people, with their property and cattle, along with them, from Magh-O'Gadhra in Cuil-O-bh-Fhinn (Coolavin), to the eastern extremity of the Coirrshliabh; for they were afraid that the English of Sligeach would plunder them in their absence, were they far distant from them. Thus they remained for some time, face to face, in readiness for each other; and many person were disabled and wounded between them, while in the monastery. The English deemed it too long they had been in that situation; and they resolved to face Bealach-Buidhe, and pass it in despite of Rudhraighe and O'Conchobhair. They were met and responded to by the Irish; and a fierce battle was fought between them, in which many of the English were slain; so that they (the survivors) were compelled to return back, after being much disheartened. They afterwards left the monastery, and returned to Rosscomain.

"Rudhraighe and O'Conchobhair proceeded across Coirrshliabh, and pitched their camp at Eas-dara, to wage war with the English of Sligeach. One day they overtook a party of the English aforementioned, who were cutting down the corn and green crops of the country, because they were not rich in provisions, and they were annihilated by them at once. They (i.e. the English of Sligeach and Rudhraighe O'Domhnaill and his party) afterwards made a month's truce with each other.

"Thus they passed the time until the beginning of winter, when the Lord Lieutenant and General of the war of Ireland (namely, Charles Blount, Lord Mountjoy) sent messengers and letters to Rudhraighe O'Domhnaill, requesting him to come upon terms of peace and tranquility. The import of these (letters) was, that it was meet for him to come upon terms of peace and friendship, and that, if he would not, he should be sorry for it, for that news had reached him that O'Domhnaill, Rudhraighe's brother, had died in Spain, and that the

123

war was at an end by his death, and that it would be a great want of wisdom, and (self) delusion, in him, if he did not make peace with him (Mountjoy) immediately.

"As soon as he had read the letters, Rudhraighe called his advisers to him, to consider what he should do; and he began to deliberate with them in council. Some of them said that the (report of) O'Domhnaill's death was not true, but that the story had been fabricated, (and sent him) to allure and deceive him (Rudhraighe), and to bind him by law. Another party asserted that the rumor was true, that it was good advice to accept of the peace, when it was requested of them; so that what they finally agreed upon was, that he and O'Conchobhair Sligeach should go to Athluain, to ratify their peace with the General. They afterwards went, and were welcomed by the General; and he showed great honor and respect to the son of O'Domhnaill, and made peace with him on behalf of the King, and confirmed his friendship with him in particular. He then recommended him to return, if he thought proper, to his patrimony.

"O'Neill (Aedh, the son of Feardorcha) and most of the Irish of Leath-Chuinn, except O'Ruaire, came in under peace; for a proclamation for a general peace, and a restoration of his blood and territory to every one that wished for it, had been issued by His Majesty King James, after he had been appointed in the place of the Queen (as King) over England, France, and Ireland.

"Mac Suibhne Fanad (Domhnaill) came under the law to join Niall O'Domhnaill.

"Mac Suibhne-na-Tuath (Maelmuire, the son of Murchadh), and Cath-bharr Og, the son of Cathbharr, son of Maghnus O'Domhnaill, went to Tirconaill, with their people and cattle, to wage war with Niall Garbh and the English. They made no delay until they arrived at the Rosses and the Islands. They had not been long here when they were plundered by Niall and his kinsmen: and Cathbharr Og was taken prisoner, and detained in custody.

"The people of Rudhraighe O'Domhnaill repaired to Tirconaill with all their property, cattle, and various effects, in the first month of spring. But Rudhraighe himself, with his gathering and muster of Irish and English, with Captain Guest, went (before his people had removed from the west) to revenge and get satisfaction of O'Ruaire (Brian Og), for the insult and dishonor he had some time before offered him (as he had in contemplation some time before); so that they plundered and ravaged Breifne, both its crops and corn, and all the cattle they could seize upon, for the greater part of them had been driven into the wilds and recesses of the territory. A few persons were slain between them, among whom were Eoghan, the son of Feardorcha O'Gallchubhair, and Toirrdhealbhach, the son of Mac Lochlainn, who fell by each other on that occasion. A party of the English were left in garrison at Drum-da-eithcar, for the purpose of plundering the country around them. O'Ruaire was thenceforward obliged to remain with a few troops in the woods or precipitous valleys, or on the islands in the lakes of his territory.

"As for Niall Garbh O'Domhnaill, a letter arrived from Dublin to him, requesting of him to come before the Lord Justice and the Council, to receive a patent for Tirconnaill, as a reward for his services and his assistance to the Crown. He neglected this thing; and what he did was, to go to Kill-meic-nenain, and send for O'Firghil, the Comharb of Colamkille; and he was styled O'Domhnaill, without consulting the King's representative or the Council. After the Lord Justice and the Council had heard of this, they became incensed against Niall, and even the General, Sir Henry Docwra, did not well like him, although he had been faithful to him, and had rendered him much service before that time.

"Rudhraighe O'Domhnaill happended to be in Dublin at this time; and he was cited to appear before the Lord Justice and the Council. Letters and writings were sent with him to Sir Henry Docwra, ordering him to take Niall Garbh prisoner. Some captains were sent in company with him; and when Rudhraighe arrived at Derry, the Governor sent a party of the officers and captains of Derry Tuathal, the son of the Dean O'Gallchubhair; Aedh Buidhe, the son of John Og; and Feilim, the son of John Og, with others besides them, were taken prisoners on that occasion, Niall Garbh made his escape shortly afterwards, and proceeded himself, with his kinsmen and people, into the woods of Keann-Maghair (now Kinnaweer in the north of Kilmacrenan parish.)

"At this time Maghnus Og O'Sruthein was killed by Domhnall, the son of Conn O'Domhnaill, in revenge of his brother, Calbhach, son of Conn, whom he (Maghnus) had slain some time before. It would have been better for him that he had not done this deed, for many evils redounded to them (his family) on account of it; for orders were given to Rudhraighe O'Domhnaill and all the Irish that were with him, to the captains who had come with him into the territory, and to Capt. Guest, who had been in his company in Connacht, to pursue Niall, his brothers and people, and to plunder and prey them. He

(Rudhraighe) did as he was ordered, so that not a single head of cattle was left with Niall's people, the others having carried off with them
several thousand head of cattle; so that vast numbers of those who
were plundered died of cold and famine. Rudhraighe divided the
preys and gave their due proportions of them to the gentlemen who
came in his army. Aedh Buidhe, the son of Conn, was wounded in
the ancle; and he was sent to Crannog-na-n-Duini in Ros-Guill, in
the Tuathas, to be healed. The same Aedh was taken prisoner by the
English, and conveyed to Derry, to be confined; and the Governor
declared that he would not liberate him until the person who committed the slaying (Domhnall, son of Conn) should come in his ram-
som. Niall and Domhnall afterwards repaired to the Governor on
parole (of honor); and Aedh Buidhe was set at liberty, and Domhnall
detained.

"Niall O'Domhnaill afterwards went to England, to solicit pardon for
his offences, and to obtain the reward for his service and aid to the
Crown of England from King James. Rudhraighe O'Domhnaill also
went to England from the same motives, although the services of both
to the Crown were very different indeed. Each of them exhibited his
right to Tirconaill. The King and Council then ordered that
Rudhraighe O'Domhnaill should be Earl over Tirconaill, and that
Niall should possess his own patrimonial inheritance, namely, that
tract of country extending from Leachta-Siubhaine, westwards, to
Seascann-Lubanach, lying on both sides of the River Finn. Both then
returned to Ireland in peace and amity, matters having been thus settled between them.

"Niall Garbh, the son of Rudhraighe, son of Egnechan, son of
Egnechan, son of Neachtan, son of Toirr-dhealbhach-an-Fhina
O'Domhnaill, died.

"An intolerable famine prevailed all over Ireland."

A.D. 1605. — "Sir Arthur Chichester, Lord Justice of Ireland, and
the Earl of Tyrone (Aedh, the son of Feardorcha), went to Srath-ban.
O'Neill claimed a portion of the territory which Niall O'Domhnaill
had obtained from the King, namely Moen-tacht. Niall produced
before the Lord Justice the proofs that he had of his right to
Moentacht, in succession from his ancestors; and, among the rest, he
produced the charters which Maghnus O'Domhnaill had obtained
from O'Neill (Conn Bacach) for setting at liberty Henry, the son of
John, whom O'Domhnaill (Maghnus) had in his custody. The Lord
Justice, Sir Arthur, having understood their stories on both sides, he

adjudged Moentacht to Niall, and said that O'Neill could not by right claim the lands, inasmuch as his title, having been more than sixty years in abeyance, had become obsolete. Both were obliged to abide by this decision."

A.D. 1606. "Meg-Uidhir (Cuconnacht) and Donnchadh, the son of Mathghamhain, son of the Bishop O'Briain, brought a ship with them to Ireland, and put in at the harbour of Suileach. They took with them from Ireland the Earl O'Neill (Aedh, the son of Feardorcha), and the Earl O'Domhnaill (Rudhraighe, the son of Aedh, son of Maghnus), with a great number of the chieftains of the province of Ulster. These were they who went with O'Neill, namely, the Countess Catherina, the daughter of Meg-Aenghusa, her three sons, Aedh the Baron, John, and Brian; Art Og, the son of Cormac, son of the Baron; Feardorcha, son of Conn, son of O'Neill; Aedh Og, the son of Brian, son of Art O'Neill; and many others of his faithful friends. These were they who went with the Earl O'Domhnaill; Cath-bharr, his brother, and his sister Nuala; Aedh, the Earl's son, wanting three weeks of being one year old; Rois, the daughter of O'Dochartaigh, and wife of Cath-bharr, with her son Aedh, aged two years and three months; the son of his brother, Domhnall Og, the son of Domhnall; Neachtain, the son of Calbhach, son of Donnchadh Cairbreach O'Domhnaill; together with many others of his faithful friends. They entered the ship on the festival of the Holy Cross, in autumn.

"This was a distinguished crew for one ship; for it is indeed certain that the sea had not supported, and the winds had not wafted from Ireland, in modern times, a party of one ship who would have been more illustrious or noble, in point of genealogy, or more renowned for deeds, valor, prowess, or high achievements, than they, if God had permitted them to remain in their patrimonies until their children should have reached the age of manhood. Woe to the heart that meditated, woe to the mind that conceived, woe to the council that decided on, the project of their setting out on this voyage, without knowing whether they should ever return to their native principalities or patrimonies to the end of the world."

A.D. 1608. "Great dissensions and strife arose between the Governor of Derry, Sir George Pawlett, and O'Dochartaigh (Cathair, the son of John Og.) The Governor not only offered him insult and abuse by word, but also inflicted chastisement on his body; so that he would rather have suffered death than live to brook such insult and dishonor, or defer or delay to take revenge for it; and he was filled with anger and fury, so that he nearly ran to distraction and madness. What he did was, to consult with his friends how he should take revenge for the insult which was inflicted upon him. What they first unanimously resolved, on the 3rd of May, was to invite to him Captain Hart, who was at Cuil-mor (a fort on the margin of Loch Foyle, below the Derry we have mentioned) and to take him prisoner. (This was done), and he obtained the fort in his release. He repaired immediately at daybreak to Derry, and awoke the soldiers of that town with the sword. The Governor was slain by Eoghan, the son of Niall, son of Gerald O'Dochartaigh, and Lieutenant Corbie by John, the son of Aedh, son of Aedh Dubh O'Domhnaill. Many others were slain besides these. Capt. Henry Vaughan and the wife of the Bishop of the town were taken prisoners. They afterwards plundered and burned the town, and carried away immense spoils from thence.

"Alas! although it was no wonder that this noble chieftain should have avenged his dishonor, innumerable and indescribable were the evils that sprang up and pullulated in the entire province of Ulster through this warlike rising, which he undertook against the King's law; for from it resulted his own death, on the 18th of July following, by the Chief Marshal of Ireland, Robert Wingfield, and Sir Oliver Lambert. He was cut into quarters between Derry and Cuil-mor, and his head was sent to Dublin, to be exhibited; and many of the gentlemen and chieftains of the province, too numerous to be particularized, were also put to death. It was indeed from it, and from the departure of the Earls we have mentioned, it came to pass that their principalities, their territories, their estates, their lands, their forts, their fortresses, their fruitful harbours, and their fishful bays, were taken from the Irish of the province of Ulster, and given in their presence to foreign tribes; and they were expelled and banished into other countries, where most of them died.

"Niall Garbh O'Domhnaill, with his brothers (Aedh Buidhe and Domhnall) and his son, Neachtain, were taken prisoners about the festival of St. John in this year, after being accused of having been in confederacy with O'Dochartaigh. They were afterwards sent to Dublin, from hence Niall and Neachtain were sent to London, and committed to the Tower, Niall having been freed from death by the decision of the law; and they (Niall and Neachtain) remained confined in the Tower to the end of their lives. Aedh and Domhnall were liberated from their captivity afterwards, i.e. in the year following.

"The Earl of Tirconnaill (Rudhraighe, son of Aedh, son of Maghnus, son of Aedh Dubh, son of Aedh Ruadh O'Domhnaill) died at Rome, on the 28th July, and was interred in the Franciscan monastery situate on the hill on which St. Peter the Apostle was crucified, after lamenting his faults and crimes, after confession, exemplary penance for his sins and transgressions, and after receiving the body and blood of Christ from the hands of the psalm-singing clergy of the Church of Rome. Sorrowful (it is to consider) the short life and early eclipse of him who was there deceased, for he was a brave, protecting, valiant, puissant, and warlike man, and had often been in the gap of danger along with his brother, Aedh Ruadh (before he himself had assumed the lordship of Tirconaill), in defence of his religion and his patrimony. He was a generous, bounteous, munificent, and truly hospitable lord, to whom the patrimony of his ancestors did not seem anything for his spending and feasting parties; and a man who did not place his mind or affections upon worldly wealth and jewels, but distributed and circulated them among all those who stood in need of them, whether the mighty or the feeble.

"Cath-bharr, son of Aedh, son of Maghnus (O'Domhnaill), a lord's son, who had borne a greater name, renown, and celebrity, for entertainment of guests and hospitality, than all who were in the Isle of Eireamon; a second Cuanna-mac-Cailchinni, and a second Guair-mac-Colmain for bounty and hospitality; and a man from (the presence of) whom no one had ever turned away with a refusal of his request; died at Rome on the 17th of September, and was buried with his brother, the Earl.

"Aedh O'Neill, the son of Aedh, son of Feardorcha, Baron of Dungannon, and the heir of the Earl O'Neill, the only expectation of the Kineal-Eoghain to succeed his father, if he had survived him, died, and was buried in the same place with his mother's brothers, the Earl O'Domhnaill and Cath-bharr."

"Cath-bharr Og, the son of Cath-bharr, son of Maghnus, Aedh Dubh O'Domhnaill, was put to death at Dublin, by the English, on the 18th of July. It would have been no disgrace to the tribe of Conall, son of Niall, to elect this good man as their chief, if he had been permitted to go home to take the leadership of them, by reason of the nobleness of his blood and the greatness of his mind and for his vigor, magnanimity, prudence, prowess, and puissance, in maintaining a battle against his opponents."

A.D. 1616. "O'Neill (Aedh, son of Feardorcha, son of Conn Bacach, son of Conn, son of Henry, son of Eoghan), who had been Baron from the death of his father to the year when the celebrated

Parliament was held in Dublin, 1584 [*recte* 1585], and who was styled Earl of Tyrone at that Parliament, and who was afterwards styled O'Neill, died at an advanced age, after having passed his life in prosperity and happiness, in valiant and illustrious achievements, in honor and nobleness. The place at which he died was Rome, (and his death occurred) on the 20th of July, after exemplary penance for his sins, and gaining the victory over the world and the devil. Although he died far from Armagh, the burial-place of his ancestors, it was a token that God was pleased with his life that the Lord permitted him a no worse burial-place, namely, Rome, the head (city) of the Christians. The person who here died was a powerful, mighty lord; (endowed) with wisdom, subtlety, and profundity of mind and intellect; a warlike, valorous, predatory, enterprising lord, in defending his religion and his patrimony against his enemies; a pious and charitable lord, mild and gentle with his friends, fierce and stern towards his enemies, until he had brought them to submission and obedience to his authority; a lord who had not coveted to possess himself of the illegal or excessive property of any other, except such as had been hereditary in his ancestors from a remote period; a lord with the authority and praiseworthy characteristics of a prince, who had not suffered theft or robbery, abduction or rape, spite or animosity, to prevail during his reign; but had kept all under (the authority of) the law, as was meet for a prince."

1  Ann. Pp. 2208, 2209, &c.

2  *To go over to them* — P. O'Sullevan states that Niall Garbh was deserted by his wife for his treachery towards her brother on this occasion. "Asper eam occasionem opportunam ratus, ad Anglos se confert (ob id a Nolla coniuge sua Odonelli sorore desertus), quibus Leffiriam, quam ipse custodiae causa tenebat, tradit. In ea Angli decem cohorts collocant." – *Hist. Cathol. &c.*, tom. 3, lib. 6, c. v fol. 171.

3  *For want of* — literally, "without sleep, without rest every night, for fear of O'Domhnaill."

4  *Of their situation* — literally, "of the place in which they were."

5  *The same loch*: i.e the same loch on which Derry is situate. The reader is to bear in mind that the Irish called all the extent of water from Lifford to the sea by the name of Loch Feabhuil. What modern mapmakers call the River Foyle, the ancient Irish considered as part of the loch.

6  *They were afraid*, literally, "fear did not permit them to leave the fort in which they were for any thing they were in need of."

7  *Cruachan-Lighean*, now Croaghan, a remarkable hill giving name to a townland in the parish of Cloncleigh, barony of Raphoe, and county of Donegal. The summit of this hill is about two miles north and by west of the bridge of Lifford. According to the Ulster Inquisitions this townland belonged to the monastery of Clonleigh. – See also the Life of St. Cairneach in Colgan's Acta Sanctorum at 28th March, p. 782, where Cruachan-Lighean is described as situate "ad occidentalem ripam freti siue sinus vulgo Loch-febhuil nuncupati, iuxta Lifferam oppidum." – See the reference to Druim Lighean which was an alias name of this place, under the years, 1522, 1524, and 1583.

8  *In want of forces* — literally, "in dearth or scarcity of forces."

9  *More of* — This idea is not very correct. It should be expressed thus: "But O'Domhnaill's people suffered more in this skirmish than the enemy, on account of the fewness of their number."

10  *Beyond the reach* — literally "where their enemies could not reach them."

11  *Dael* — now Deel, or, as it is called by the descendants of the Scotch settlers, Daleburn, a river which flows through the barony of Raphoe, and discharges itself into the Foyle a short distance to the north of the town of Lifford — See note e, under the year 1557, p. 1557.

12  *The steed* — The Four Masters should have omitted this short sentence, which so much incumbers their narrative. P. O'Sullevan Beare, who had wooed the historic Muse with more success than any of the Four Masters, describes this battle much more elegantly, as follows, in his *Hist. Cathol. Iber. Compend.*, tom. 3, lib. 6, c.v.: "Erat Asper vir animo magno, & audaci, & rei militaris scientia praeditus, atque multos a sua parte Tirconellos habebat, quorum opera, & virtute fretus in plano cum Catholicis manum conserere non recusabat: Fidem tamen Ctholicam semper retinuit Haereticorum ceremonias auersatus, sicut & Artus (Onellus) qui cito e vita discessit. Circum Leffriam vero, & Lucum a regijs & Catholicis acriter & saepe dimicatum est. Memorabilis est equestris pugna, qua regijs fugatis Magnus Odonelli frater Asperum loco cedentem hasta transfossurus fuisset, nisi eius ictum remoueret Eugenius Ogallachur cognomento Iunior ipsius Magni Comes pietate & amore in Onellam suorum dominorum familaim motus. In quam familiam dispari animo fuit Cornelius Ogallachur, qui Aspero persuasisse fertur, vt ad Anglos faceret transitionem, & Magnum vulnerauit apud Moninem iuxta Leffiriam, vbi equitatus vtrinque incomposite concurrit, & Magnus equo vectus interquinque equites Ibernos regios ab Aspero in dextero latere hasta percutitur, & circumuentus a Cornelio sub humero icitur. Hastarum cuspides licet loricam non penetrauerint tamen Magno in corpus infixerunt. Rothericus fratri auxilio veniens Asperi pectus hasta appetit; Asper loris, tractis equi eaput tollens eius fronte excipit Rotherici ictum, quo equus fixus exanimis cum aspero corruit. Sed Asper a suis leuatus Leffriam reuertitur, Odonello cum peditibus appropinquante. Magnus ex vulneribus egit animan intra decimum quintum diem, & breui Cornelius ab Odonello deprehensus laqueo strangulatur." — Fol. 171, 172.

13  *Their leader* — This was Captain Heath. "He tooke a shott in the thigh whereof he shortlie after died." —*Docwra.*

14  *The son of their chief* — His father Aedh, was still living, but was not the chief ruler of Tirconnell at the time, for he had resigned to his eldest son, Aedh Ruadh, as early as the year 1592, when it is stated by the Four Masters that he was old and feeble. — See p. 1929.

15  *Sons of Life* — i.e. religious persons. It is the antithesis of *meic bain* i.e. sons or children of death, which means Malefactors, or wicked or irreligious persons.

16  *Confessors* — *Anmchairde* is the plural of *Anmchara* or *Anamchara*, which is translated "confessarius" by Colgan in his *Trias Thaum.* p. 294, and "synedrus seu confessarius" at p. 298. The term literally signifies "friend of the soul," and is used in ancient Irish writings in the sense of spiritual director or father confessor.

17  Of *Inbhirmor, Inbhir mór, Portus magnus*, now Broad Haven, in the north of the barony of Erris, and county of Mayo. Docwra says that these ships put in at Calebeg, now Killybegs.

18  *Kealla-beaga* — See this place already referred to under the years 1513, 1516, 1550. Now Killybegs.

19  *Dun-Neill* — i.e. the Dun or Fort of Niall, now Dunneill, *alias* Castlequarter, a townland in the parish of Kilmacshalgan, barony of Tireragh, and county of Sligo.

— See *Genealogies, Tribes, &c., of Ui-Fiachrach*, pp. 134, 135, 171, 175, 262, 305, 306, and the map to the same work.

20 *Harbour of Teilinn*, now Teelin, a small harbour about a mile and a half long, but very narrow, situate about seven miles westwards of Killybegs, in the barony of Banagh, and county of Donegal.

# CHRONOLOGY

## 1600

### APRIL

28 April     English force rendezvous at Carrickfergus.

### MAY

7 May     Fleet sails for Lough Foyle.

14 May     Fleet arrives in Lough Foyle but runs aground on sandbanks.

16 May     English force is attacked as it lands at Culmore. Docwra orders the construction of a fort at Culmore.

c. 18 May     The English occupy Elaghmore castle.

22 May     Derry is taken without incident and occupied. Two forts are constructed to house the garrrison.

29 May     Sir John Chamberlain attacks the west bank of the Foyle.

### JUNE

1 June     Sir Art Ó Néill joins the English force at Derry.

2 June     On Sir Art's advice Docwra garrisons Elaghmore.

10 June     Docwra orders an attack by boat from Greencastle on the lordship of Ó Catháin in County Londonderry.

29 June     Muintir Uí Dhochartaigh attack Elaghmore. Sir John Chamberlain is killed. Docwra's horse is shot and killed while he is trying to rescue Chamberlain.

### JULY

2 July     The English capture and garrison Dunnalong under Sir John Bolles.

14 July     Ó Domhnaill skirmishes with the English near Dunnalong.

29 July     Ó Domhnaill's forces seize most of the English horses.

Docwra counter-attacks immediately but is seriously wounded.

## AUGUST

Early August  Maol Mhuire Mac Suibhne na dTuath escapes from an English ship at Derry.

24 August  Ruaidhrí Ó Catháin parleys with Docwra and offers to serve him. Docwra realises that this is merely a ruse. He hangs some of Muintir Chatháin.

## SEPTEMBER

16 September An Irish night attack is repulsed with no loss to the garrison.

17 September The English garrison is resupplied.

## OCTOBER

3 October  Niall Garbh Ó Domhnaill joins with Docwra.

4 October  The English attack Inch Island in Inishowen.

8 October  Docwra sends Niall Garbh with Sir John Bolles to take Lifford.

11 October  Ó Domhnaill camps near Lifford at Castlefin.

25 October  Ó Domhnaill's troops are repulsed by the Lifford garrison.

## NOVEMBER

10 November Ó Domhnaill withdraws from Lifford to rendezvous with Aodh Ó Néill, Earl of Tyrone, and recently arrived Spanish vessels at Killybegs.

## DECEMBER

Christmas  Death of Sir Seán Ó Dochartaigh; Docwra's troops dig-in for the winter.

# 1601

MARCH

End of March Docwra attacks Clann tSuibhne in Fanad. They promise allegiance. (In the following September Clann tSuibhne again attacked the English garrison and again surrendered after another attack by Docwra.) Captain Ralph Bingley garrisons Rathmullan Abbey.

Ash Wednesday
The Bishop of Derry is taken and killed by Sir Henry Bolles.

APRIL

April     Docwra moves against Muintir Uí Néill in Tyrone; Castlederg is delivered up to him by Niall Garbh; the English await resupply from England to mount a summer campaign.

April–May     The English construct a chain of forts across the southern end of Lough Swilly from Carrigans to Coelmackatren (Castleforward) to cut off Inishowen from raids by Ó Domhnaill.

MAY

7 May     800 men arrive as reinforcements. Docwra defeats Ó Domhnaill near Coelmackatren.

24 May     Newtownstewart is captured after bombardment, and garrisoned by Captain Roger Atkinson.

JUNE

20 June     Docwra attacks the Ó Catháin castle at Enagh Lough. Receives orders to assist the Lord Deputy in capturing Ballyshannon.

21 June     Enagh is taken after the garrison flees.

JULY

19 July     Further letters arrive ordering Docwra to meet the Lord Deputy at the Blackwater. Sir Henry discovers his troops have no match and cannot risk a march through enemy territory.

AUGUST

2 August    Docwra rescues his reputation by sending Niall Garbh and 500 English troops to capture the Abbey of Donegal.

6 August    The Derry garrison is resupplied with match from Sir Arthur Chichester at Carrickfergus.

SEPTEMBER

19 September During an attack by Ó Domhnaill, Donegal Abbey is destroyed.

mid-September
                Newtownstewart and Castlederg are taken by Irish forces. The garrison at Newtownstewart is put to the sword; the Castlederg garrison escapes.

21 September Spanish forces under Don Juan del Aguila arrive at Kinsale in Co. Cork. Ó Néill and Ó Domhnaill march south to meet them.

September–November
                Docwra raids Fanad again after Clann tSuibhne join Ó Domhnaill. After the departure of Ó Domhnaill's troops Docwra seizes the opportunity to attack Muintir Uí Catháin.

DECEMBER

12 December The garrison at Donegal is resupplied from Derry; Ashrowe (Assaroe) Abbey is garrisoned.

24 December The Irish and Spanish are heavily defeated at Kinsale by Lord Deputy Mountjoy; Aodh Ruadh Ó Domhnaill leaves for Spain to seek further help and dies soon after. Rudhraighe succeeds to the chieftainship.

# 1602

## MARCH

25 March    Docwra's men, under the command of Captain Digges, capture Ballyshannon.

## APRIL

20 April    Dungiven Castle is delivered to Docwra by Cú Mhaighe Ballach mac Riocaird Uí Cathaín.

## MAY

End of May    800 reinforcements arrive from England; Docwra is summoned to meet Lord Deputy Mountjoy.

## JUNE

16 June    Docwra sets out from Lifford to meet Mountjoy; he fortifies Omagh, which is garrisoned by Captain Edmond Leigh.

26 June    Docwra meets the Lord Deputy at Dungannon.

27 June    Sir Arthur Chichester establishes a fort on Lough Neagh; Mountjoy erects Charlemont fort.

## JULY

6 July    Docwra returns to Derry.

27 July    Muintir Chatháin submit to Docwra.

## NOVEMBER

18 November Docwra moves to join Chichester in attacking Aodh Ó Néill.

Rudhraighe Ó Domhnaill surrenders to Mountjoy.

## DECEMBER

18–23 December

Using Dungannon as his base, Docwra attacks Ó Néill; his Irish troops mutiny; the English plan miscarries when Chichester's and Docwra's troops fail to rendezvous.

# 1603

### JANUARY

January — Niall Garbh and Docwra part company over Niall's claim to the title of the Ó Domhnaill; Sir Henry has him arrested. Niall Garbh escapes but is recaptured in Fanad.

### MARCH

24 March — Death of Elizabeth I, accession of James VI and I.

30 March — Aodh Ó Néill, earl of Tyrone, surrenders to Lord Deputy Mountjoy. Treaty of Mellifont.

Docwra goes to Dublin to meet the Lord Deputy. He carries the hopes and petitions of the Irish with him. Those who had assisted the English now appeal to Docwra to protect them from the restored earls.

### APRIL

Niall Garbh escapes from Derry, but is recaptured.

### LATER EVENTS

1604 — Charter of the City of Derry is granted by James I. Docwra is appointed Provost for life, clerk of the markets and King's Admiral.

1606 — (July) Docwra leaves Derry; sells his interest to Sir William Wilson; is replaced by Sir George Paulet.

1607 — Flight of the Earls.

1608 — Docwra is appointed to the Commission for Irish Causes; Sir Cathaír Ó Dochartaigh captures and burns Derry.

1616 — Docwra is appointed Treasurer at War in Ireland.

1621 — Docwra is created Baron of Culmore.

1627 — Docwra is appointed Joint Keeper of the Great Seal of Ireland.

1631 — Sir Henry Docwra dies and is buried at Christchurch Cathedral, Dublin.

# GLOSSARY

The text of the Narration is not difficult to read. Docwra's voluminous letters are testimony to his fondness for writing and his ability to express himself. The reader will be well rewarded for the small effort required to become familiar with Docwra's spelling, which is not idiosyncratic but rather follows the conventions of his times. Nevertheless, this short glossary has been provided to assist the reader with terms used by Docwra that are not in common use today. A few notes on Docwra's most common techniques might also help.

Like his seventeenth-century contemporaries, Docwra spelt phonetically.

O'Donovan transcribed the text correctly and therefore used 'u' for 'v' as was the custom of the time, as in 'braue' for 'brave.'

The 'y' at the end of a word was often rendered as 'ie', as in 'presentlie'.

| | |
|---|---|
| alarume | alarm |
| allighted | dismounted |
| aquavitae | whiskey |
| aduertised | warned, alerted, informed |
| aucthoritie | authority |
| battaile | battle |
| bawne (bawn) | a house fortified with a wall, towers, and sometimes a ditch |
| biskitt/biskett | rations composed mainly of hard tack |
| beeues (beeves) | cattle (the measure of wealth among the Irish) |
| bewraying | revealing |
| capassitie | capacity |
| carraige | behaviour, demeanour, manner |
| centynell | sentinel, guard |
| cessed | taxed, billeted upon |
| churles | farm-workers/peasants |
| corpes de guard | life guards |
| creaghts (creaghtes) | guarded herds of livestock |
| culverin | long-barrelled artillery weapon |
| custodium | licence |
| defensuive | defensive |
| demy (demi-culverin) | *see* culverin |

| | |
|---|---|
| dispacht | kill |
| diuers (divers) | several |
| ennuie | envy |
| entertaynement | salary, wages |
| ffoote | infantry, foot-soldiers |
| fortneth | fortnight |
| fower | four |
| garrans | Irish ponies or horses |
| graunte | grant |
| horse | cavalry |
| howses | houses |
| iniurie | injury, insult |
| kerne, kearne | lightly armed soldiers |
| lord deputie | the representative of the Crown in Ireland: at the time of Docwra the lord deputy was Lord Mountjoy and later Sir Arthur Chichester |
| lords of the councell | the English privy council |
| match | cord soaked in melted sulphur, required to fire the matchlock muskets carried by Docwra's troops |
| mayne | main |
| meale | corn |
| men of warre | warships |
| murther | murder |
| natiues | indigenous Irish |
| perswation | persuasion |
| rancke | rank |
| simplicitie | naivety |
| skowts | scouts |
| soddaynenesse | suddenness |
| spente | used, consumed |
| spoyle | raid, loot |
| stealthes | surprise attacks |
| supriced | surprised, caught unawares |
| targetts | shields |
| tearmes | terms |
| tennements | tenements |
| tryall | trial |
| vaunt guard | advance guard |
| victuells | supplies of food and drink |

**Names of persons**
Names have been given in classical modern Irish. Common orthological
variants are given in parenthesis. For example, the Irish form of the name
*Cahir* is given here as Cathaír. Historically the final vowel was long.
However, a variant form *Cathir* with a short i developed. Either form
would be equally acceptable.

| | |
|---|---|
| Seán (Seaan) Ó Néill | Shane O'Neill |
| Niall Garbh Ó Domhnaill | Neal Garve O'Donnell |
| Ó Ruairc | O'Rourke |
| Sir Seán Ó Dochartaigh | Sir Sean O'Dougherty |
| Aodh Buidhe Mac Daibhéid | Hugh Boy McDavitt |
| Sir Cathaír Ó Dochartaigh | Sir Cahir O'Dougherty |
| Ó Catháin | O'Kane |
| Sir Art Ó Néill | Sir Arthur O'Neill |
| Réamonn Ó Gallchobhair | Redmond O'Gallagher |
| Rudhraighe (Ruaidhrí) Ó Domhnaill | Rory O'Donnell |
| Maghnus Ó Domhnaill | Manus O'Donnell |
| Toirrdhealbhach (Luineach) Ó Néill | Tirlough O'Neill |
| Neachtan Ó Domhnaill | Naughten O'Donnell |
| Aodh Ruadh Ó Domhnaill | Red Hugh O'Donnell |
| Mac Suibhne Fánad | McSwine of Fanad |
| Cú Mhaighe Ballach mac Riocaird Uí Chatháin | Caue Ballogh mac Rickard |
| Aodh Mór Ó Néill | Hugh 'The Great' O'Neill |
| Feidhlim (Féilim) Óg Ó Dochartaigh | Phelim O'Doherty |
| Feidhlim (Féilim) Ruadh Mac Daibhéid | Phelim McDaid |

**Place and Population Names**

| | |
|---|---|
| Clann Dálaigh | The O'Donnells of Tír Chonaill |
| Muintir Uí Dhomhnaill | The O'Donnells and their retainers |
| Muintir Dhochartaigh | The O'Dohertys |
| Muintir Uí Dhochartaigh | The O'Dohertys and their retainers |
| Cenél Eoghain | The O'Neills and their territory in Tír Eoghain |
| Clann Daibhéid | The McDavitts |
| Muintir Chatháin | The O'Kanes of the barony of Keenaght, Co. Derry |
| Muintir Uí Chatháin | The O'Kanes and their retainers |
| Clann tSuibhne | The McSweeneys |

# BIBLIOGRAPHY

PRINTED PRIMARY SOURCES

For a full account of manuscript sources on Docwra, see HAYES, RICHARD J., *Manuscript Sources for the History of Irish Civilization* (Dublin, 1965–1979).

*Calendar of State Papers, Ireland, 1599–1600* (London, 1899).

*Calendar of State Papers, Ireland, 1600* (London, 1903).

*Calendar of State Papers, Ireland, 1600–1601* (London, 1905).

*Calendar of State Papers, Ireland, 1600–1603* (London, 1912).

*Annala Rioghachta Eireann: Annals of the Kingdom of Ireland by the Four Masters from the earliest period to the year 1616*, ed. John O'Donovan. (Dublin, 1848). See particularly vols V–VII (1501–1616).

*Calendar of the Carew Manuscripts Preserved in the Archiepiscopal Library at Lambeth*, edited by J.S. Brewer and William Bullen, 6 vols. (London, 1867–73).

DAVIES, SIR JOHN. *A discovery of the true causes why Ireland was never entirely subdued and brought under the obedience of the crown of England until the beginning of His Majesty's happy reign* (1612), ed. James P. Myers, Jr (Washington, 1988).

DOCWRA, H., 'A narration of the services done by the army ymployed to Lough Foyle', ed. John O'Donovan, *Miscellany of the Celtic Society* (Dublin, 1849).

DOCWRA, H., 'Relation', ed. John O'Donovan, *Miscellany of the Celtic Society* (Dublin, 1849).

GAINSFORD, THOMAS, *The true, exemplary and remarkable history of the earl of Tyrone* (London, 1619).


HISTORICAL MANUSCRIPTS COMMISSION REPORTS

*Fourth report*, appendix, *Mostyn MSS* (London, 1874).

*Report on the Salisbury MSS*, parts IX–XIV (London, 1902–1923).

*Second report, Fortescue MSS* (Dublin, 1874).

*HMC Various Collections*, vol. I (London, 1901).

*Third report*, appendix, *House of Lords MSS* (London, 1872).

MORYSON, F., *An History of Ireland, From the Year 1599 to 1603*, 2 vols (London 1617; reprint Dublin, 1735). See also, *The Irish sections of Fynes Moryson's unpublished Itinerary*, ed. Graham Kew (Dublin, Irish Manuscripts Commission, 1998).

MORYSON, F., *An Itinerary containing his ten yeeres travel through Germany ... England, Scotland and Ireland*, 4 vols (Glasgow, 1907–8).


SECONDARY SOURCES

ANDREWS, J. H., 'An early map of Inishowen', *Long Room, the Bulletin of the Friends of the Library of Trinity College, Dublin*, no. 7 (1973) pp. 19–25.

ANDREWS, K. R., NICHOLAS P. CANNY and P. E. H. BLAIR (eds), *The Westward Enterprise: English Activities in Ireland, the Atlantic and America* (Liverpool, 1978).

BAGWELL, R., *Ireland under the Tudors: With a Succinct Account of the Earlier History*, 3 vols (London, 1885–90).

BARDON, J., *A History of Ulster* (Belfast, 1992).

BONNER, B., 'Reamann O Gallachair, Bishop of Derry', *Donegal Annual*, IX, no. 1, 1974, pp. 41–52.

BONNER, B., *That Audacious Traitor* (Dublin, 1975).

BRADY, C., 'The Captain's games, army and society in Elizabethan Ireland,' in Bartlett, T., and Jeffery, K., *A Military History of Ireland*, pp. 136–59 (Cambridge, 1996).

BRADY, C. and GILLESPIE, R., *Natives and Newcomers: Essays on the Making of Irish Colonial Society, 1534–1641* (Dublin, 1986).

CANNY, N.P., 'The treaty of Mellifont and the reorganisation of Ulster, 1603', *Irish Sword*, IX (1969), pp. 249–62.

CANNY, N.P., 'The Flight of the Earls 1607', *Irish Historical Studies*, vol. 17, no. 67 (March 1971).

CANNY, N.P., *From Reformation to Restoration: Ireland 1534–1660* (Dublin, 1987).

CONNOLLY, S.J. (ed.), *The Oxford Companion to Irish History* (Oxford, 1998).

ELLIS, S.G., *Tudor Ireland* (London, 1985).

FALLS, C., *The Birth of Ulster* (London, 1936).

FALLS, C., *Elizabeth's Irish Wars* (London, 1950).

FALLS, C., *Mountjoy, Elizabethan General* (London, 1955).

HAYES-McCOY, G.A., *Scots Mercenary Forces in Ireland, 1565–1603* (Dublin and London, 1937).

HAYES-McCOY, G.A., 'The army of Ulster, 1593–1601', *Irish Sword*, I (1949–53), pp. 105–17.

HAYES-McCOY, G.A., *Ulster and Other Irish Maps, c.1600* (Dublin, 1964).

HAYES-McCOY, G.A., *Irish Battles: A Military History of Ireland* (London, 1969).

HAYES-McCOY, G.A., 'Conciliation, coercion, and the protestant reformation, 1547–1571', in Moody, T.W., F.X. Martin and F.J. Byrne (eds), *A New History of Ireland*, vol. III (Oxford, 1976), chapter 3, pp. 69–92.

HUNTER, R.J., 'Plantation in Donegal', in Nolan, W., Ronayne, L., and Dunlevy, M. (eds.), *Donegal, History and Society*, (Dublin, 1995) pp. 283–324.

JONES, F.M., *Mountjoy, 1563–1606, the Last Elizabethan Deputy* (Dublin, 1958).

LACY, B., *Siege City, the Story of Derry and Londonderry* (Belfast, 1990).

McCAVITT, J., *Sir Arthur Chichester, Lord Deputy of Ireland, 1605–1616* (Belfast, 1998).

McGURK, J., 'Casualties and welfare measures for the sick and wounded of the Nine Years War in Ireland, 1594–1603', in *Journal of the Society for Army Historical Research*, vol. 68 (1990), pp. 22–35, 188–204.

McGURK, J., 'The dead, sick and wounded of the Nine Years War (1594–1603)', in *History Ireland*, vol. III, no. 4 (1995), pp. 16–22.

McGURK, J., *The Elizabethan Conquest of Ireland: the 1590s Crisis* (Manchester, 1997).

McGURK, J., in Lenihan, P. (ed.), *Conquest and Resistance: War in Seventeenth Century Ireland* (Brill, 2001).

MEEHAN, C.P., *The Fate and Fortunes of the Earl of Tyrone and Rory O'Donel, Earl of Tyrconnel* (Dublin, 1868).

MILLIGAN, C.D., *The Walls of Derry, Their Building, Defending and Preserving*, 2nd edn (Belfast, 1996).

MOODY, T.W., F.X. MARTIN and F.J. BYRNE (eds), *A New History of Ireland*, vol. 3, *Early Modern Ireland, 1534–1691*, 2nd edn (Oxford, 1978).

MORGAN, H., 'The end of Gaelic Ulster: a thematic interpretation of events between 1574 and 1610', in *Irish Historical Studies*, vol. 26, no. 191 (May 1988).

MORGAN, H., *Tyrone's Rebellion: the Outbreak of the Nine Years War in Tudor Ireland* (Woodbridge, 1993).

MULLIN, T.H., *Ulster's Historic City, Derry, Londonderry* (Coleraine, 1986).

MULLIN, T.H. and J.E. MULLAN, *The Ulster Clans* (Belfast, 1966).

NEWMAN, PETER R., *Companion to Irish History, from the Submission of Tyrone to Partition, 1603–1921* (Oxford and New York, 1991).

NOLAN, W., L. RONAYNE and M. DUNLEVY (eds), *Donegal, History and Society* (Dublin, 1995).

Ó DOMHNAILL, S., 'Sir Niall Garbh O'Donnell and the rebellion of Sir Cahir O'Doherty', *Irish Historical Studies*, vol. 3, no. 9 (March 1942), pp. 34–8.

O'DONOVAN, J., *Letters containing information relative to the antiquities of Donegal collected during the progress of the Ordnance Survey in 1835* (Lifford, 1846).

Ó FAOLÁIN, S., *The Great O'Neill* (reprint, Dublin, 1981).

O'FLANAGAN, M., Rev., *Letters containing information relative to the Antiquities of the County of Donegal collected during the progress of the Ordnance Survey in 1835* (Bray, 1927).

QUINN, D.B., *The Elizabethans and the Irish* (New York, 1966).

ROBINSON, P., *The Plantation of Ulster: British Settlement in an Irish Landscape, 1600–70*, (Dublin, 1984).

SILKE, J.J., *Kinsale: the Spanish intervention in Ireland at the End of the Elizabethan Wars* (Liverpool, 1970).

SIMPSON, R., *The Annals of Derry* (reprint, Limavady, 1987).

THOMAS, A., *The Walled Towns of Ireland*, 2 vols (Dublin, 1992).

# INDEX